The **Disobedient** Indian

THE
DISOBEDIENT INDIAN

Towards a Gandhian Philosophy
of Dissent

Ramin Jahanbegloo

SPEAKING
TIGER

SPEAKING TIGER PUBLISHING PVT. LTD
4381/4, Ansari Road, Daryaganj
New Delhi-110002

First published in hardback by Speaking Tiger 2018

ISBN: 978-93-88070-34-8
eISBN: 978-93-87693-43-2

10 9 8 7 6 5 4 3 2 1

Typeset in Sabon Roman by SŪRYA, New Delhi
Printed at Sanat Printers, Kundli

To my heretic friend Ashis Nandy

CONTENTS

FOREWORD

Ramin Jahanbegloo is an active philosopher who concerns himself not only with the ultimate issues that mankind faces, but also with what is happening in the world today. This is not an isolated meditation: he is deeply concerned with the here and now of reality, of life as it is shaping itself in our rather troubled and challenging times. He is equally aware that the Western way of looking at the world is not the only way, dominant as it is; he takes into account the other ways of engaging with the ultimate and eternal questions as well as their concrete contemporary manifestations. An Iranian, imprisoned for his radical views in his own country, he now divides his time teaching between India and Canada.

In this new book, *The Disobedient Indian*, Ramin Jahanbegloo explores in depth 'a Gandhian Philosophy of Dissent' for our times. Gandhi never presented himself as a philosopher, much less as a political philosopher. Yet through his life, his actions and articulations, he expresses a radical critique of modernity, democracy, politics and the modern State. This critique offers many insights and new directions which can be seen as relevant for our contemporary dilemmas and philosophical impasse.

To arrive at the Gandhian moment of dissent and disobedience, Ramin Jahanbegeloo traverses a long path of philosophical consideration. From Aristotle to Hannah Arendt, Cornelius Castoriadis, Wilhelm Reich, Karl Jaspers and Erich Fromm—an impressive number of Western thinkers are summoned, in a manner of speaking, to address the issues of freedom, democratic behaviour, violence, truth, conformism, dissent and questioning. The overriding context is the contemporary world and its politics. A sharp analysis reveals how the most dominant forms of socio-political mobilization, institutions and modes of social conduct are promoting the 'idea of the institutionalization of un-doubt'. He adds: 'This reign of un-doubt in contemporary society is where no claims to truth come under suspicion with respect to their ontological grounds and socio-political side-effects. This has become a standard definition of human essence in a meaningless world of liberal conformism.' Ramin sets out to argue that 'a critical take on democratic thought and action can fuel a keener perception and analysis of a citizen ethos that fosters an imaginative agonism against all forms of complacency and conservatism.'

In a brilliant analysis of democracy, Ramin suggests that 'dissent, more than being a simple manner of protesting, is an invitation to awareness. Through its art of questioning, the real task of dissent is to challenge and defeat the twin corruptions of democracy: imposed conformism and normalized complacency.' As Vaclav Havel affirms: 'The intellectual should constantly disturb, should bear witness to the misery of the world, should be provocative by being independent, should rebel against all hidden and open pressure and manipulations, should be the chief doubter of systems, of power and its incantations, should be a witness to their mendacity.'

Ramin continues to describe the disobedient mind as creating 'a new grammar for itself in philosophy, art and politics. This grammar is based on a "breakthrough" from the passivity of the perpetually renewed sameness.'

Ramin makes an interesting distinction between the two concepts of the 'political' and 'politics'. According to him 'the political is the space of autonomous action of human beings in a historic context, while politics is the space of competition and contestation for the very basis of power and authority.' He believes that 'the political brings us together, where politics divides us', and he underlines that 'though not a disinterested act, the political is always collective and in a spirit of solidarity.' He recalls that 'the idea of the political got lost in the massification of politics. The overtaking of the political by contemporary crowds, both in totalitarian and democratic contexts, goes hand in hand with the loss of the instinctive reflexes for freedom and the rise of what we call the "lumpen politics".' Ramin is alert enough to point out that 'contemporary liberal theories reformulate the concept of freedom in terms of negative liberty without focusing necessarily on a fuller account of freedom as self-questioning, self-invention and determination. As a result, citizens are safeguarded from illiberal forms of interference by a system of rights, but they do not feel the urge to participate in an unregulated public space, where we can find a confrontation of ideas.'

As Ramin wisely identifies, 'one of the main weaknesses of contemporary politics is the lack of courage and outspokenness.' Pointing to the emergence of crowds as a decisive phenomenon, he notes that, 'Strangely, the crowd is never ruled by itself, but is guided and governed by a few. Crowds become habituated to modes of non-thinking and non-questioning, even about the most simplistic and trivial commonplace issues. Being diverted by bread and circus, they lose their autonomy and creativity and become incapable of looking beyond appearances.' Ramin is clearly of the view that the act of questioning is a political practice, endorsing the Kantian view that we have to take a path of moral cultivation 'to prepare ourselves for freedom' without taking it for granted. With Castoriadis, Ramin believes that 'we all have the capacity to disobey conformism and to be autonomous.' He makes a fervent plea that 'we should not prohibit, debar and exclude dissenters and wish them away from public space. Most often, heretics and dissenters have been the creative spirits of history. They have been a prime source of resistance to thoughtlessness and meaninglessness in human societies.'

Having laid a well-argued space for dissent and disobedience, Ramin moves on, almost naturally, to Gandhi, the arch dissenter of the twentieth century. He points out that 'Gandhi is one of the rare thinkers of modernity who does not follow the idea of consent as a common justification of political obligation,' because according to Gandhi, 'the moral duty of citizens, as a condition of good governance, is not seen in the act of continuous legitimation of the State. In a deeper sense...the democratic citizen owes its final allegiance to its own capacity of self-government.' He finds that the 'Gandhian legitimation of disobedience through the widening of boundaries of citizenship are only ways to remind the citizens that the political process which decides whether an act of disobedience is right or wrong is not infallible.' Gandhi emphasizes that 'the political is founded on the basic idea that both legality and the act of disobeying it need to be grounded in truth (satya) and involve practice of virtue.' Ramin also underlines that, for Gandhi, 'the act of disobedience is to improve the quality of justice in a society by upgrading the moral temper of social and political institutions.'

For Gandhi, the idea of disobedience was an innovative one, for it was 'not only a critique of authority, but also a revolution of values.' For him, 'disobedience, as a spirit and as an act has an ethical significance more than just a tactical value in non-violent struggle.' While reminding us of the 'inherent fragility of human existence and the frailty of the human political condition,' Ramin finds 'Gandhi is very conscious about the fact that cultivation of an "enlarged pluralism" requires the creation of institutions and practices where the voice and perspective of everyone can be articulated, tested and transformed.' Ramin forcefully adds, 'As such, Gandhi still has the disturbing capacity to unsettle our fixed habits and let us see world in a new light.' Indeed, this book succeeds in making us see the poetics of disobedience in the utterly illiberal prosaic ethos of our times, in the light of giving Gandhi a new radical and transformative significance.

ASHOK VAJPEYI
New Delhi, 2018

INTRODUCTION

THE OBLIGATION TO DISOBEY

This book explores and engages with one of the most difficult challenges any individual or society could face: the problem of disobedience, whether expressed in theory or in action, as a necessary mode of thinking and acting in a thoughtless and complacent world, where the legitimate praxis of self-creation and self-transformation of the individual and her disobedience of the law invites punishment and prosecution. In other words, disobedience may appear to many as an unrealistic and unjustifiable method of argumentation and social action, and a subversive vision of legality. But in order to discuss the problem of disobedience more soundly and strongly, it must be treated as part of a larger panorama, which not only fosters practices of freedom and autonomy, but also involves an ongoing questioning of the political norms and moods. In the pages that follow, we will explore in the first part of the book the formulation of disobedience throughout history, while in the second part we will take a detailed look into Gandhi's philosophy and practice of disobedience.

Quite obviously, when we think in terms of dissent and disobedience, we aspire to a harmonious exchange among agents of the political, in contrast to the theoretical and practical justifications of social inequalities that engender considerable unevenness of power. As a result, to be disobedient is to not only to practice self-development and self-transformation as one's own preferences, but also to tackle the shortcomings of the preferences themselves. This is the point where critical thinking and dissentful acting are blended outside the 'iron cage', to refer to a term coined by Max Weber and pointing to a system of rational calculation and control. As a matter of fact, the disobedient mind owes allegiance to nothing and nobody but the challenges of thinking and acting; the two ways of re-examining the relation between freedom and common life. Therefore, none of us can dismiss the fact that the idea of disobedience has the greatest consequences for our present-day world and for the future of humanity. Far from being an invitation to chaos and violence, disobedience is a constructive and creative attitude in pursuit of a self-reflecting and non-conformist community.

In a deeper sense, it is a serious and conscientious commitment to explore new vistas of change and exchange for our common life, in a time when populism and mass immaturity are holding each other in sway. This is where a look back at the Gandhian philosophy of resistance becomes a call to political wisdom. As such, anyone interested in fighting political injustice and social inequality, but also motivated to go beyond the mental ghettos that create the complacent and conformist attitudes toward political injustice and social inequality, feels compelled to ask about Mahatma Gandhi's contribution to the art of dissent and to the philosophy of disobedience.

In a way, this book is another attempt to search and understand Gandhi's valuable art of disobeying. But it is, at the same time, a quest for the last resort of critical thinking in our civilization of calculation and utility, at a time when, for many around the world, mediocrity has become a norm of living and violence a mode of dying. No doubt, there are certain concepts and modes of action that the disobedient mind must hold clearly and truly in order to replace contemporary averageness by a commitment to self-examination. As such, maybe disobedience and dissent are the only strategies and instruments left to our distracted society to bring its hidden mediocrity to the surface. Gandhi held that every citizen is responsible for every act of the State. This is the most extreme act of disloyalty in modern politics. It destroys our habits of willing obedience to the State, but it also changes the whole definition of a law-abiding citizen.

Gandhi was well aware of the difficulty of this task from his own experience. He was disappointed by his whole political experience in India. What was a tragic disappointment to him has become a snobbish arrogance to today's politicians. Gandhi's disobedience has been easily abused, especially by those who cast doubts on the moral dignity of the political against the crippling sense of docility in everyday politics. But on the whole, the disobedient Indian exemplifies the universality of disobedience as a moral and intellectual necessity in our world.

Also, let us not forget that the history of political thought began with an act of disobedience, that of Socrates—the Athenian philosopher and gadfly—against his judges who condemned him to death; but it is unlikely that it will end by an act of obedience. As long as human beings have the mental capacity and the moral courage to question ideas, actions and institutions, which they have thought and constituted socio-historically, the value of disobedience is assessed largely as a matter of human freedom. More importantly, all theoretical interrogation about the nature of the political is based on the premise of the existence of a disobedient mind as the only true criterion of what is right or wrong, or just or unjust. As Henry David Thoreau, one of the greatest influences on Gandhi's practise of disobedience, declares, 'The only obligation which I have a right to assume, is to do at any time what I think right.'[1] The right to disobey is, according to Thoreau, a duty of the individual conscience. This rebellious quality, however, is not only an act of questioning reality, but also a moral self-restraint from doing the wrong and the unjust. In other words, in Thoreau's eyes, 'What I have to do is to see, at any rate, that I do not lend myself to the wrong which I condemn.'[2]

If freedom is the most basic and general principle of human needs, then the right to disobey must be the right to optimal protection against the enslavement of freedom. As George Woodcock asserts, 'While there are still men who disobey in the name of justice and decency, humanity is not enslaved.' And he adds, 'When the duty to obey without question is accepted, that is the moment of freedom's death.'[3] But for people who worry less about freedom of thought and thinking freedom and are more concerned with security and order, questioning and disobeying are not urgent matters in life. This, too, is an argument that Thoreau laid down in clear philosophical terms in his essay while trying to explain and justify the opposite. As he puts it, 'Unjust laws exist: shall we be content to obey them, or shall we endeavour to amend them, and obey them until we have succeeded, or shall we transgress them at once? Men generally, under such a government as this, think they ought to wait until they have persuaded the majority to alter them. They think that, if they should resist, the remedy would be worse than the evil. But it is the fault of the government itself that the remedy *is* worse than the evil. It makes it worse.'[4] What Thoreau is condemning herewith is the tacit consent of the citizens which disallows the possibility of any legitimate moral resistance against the political establishment. He, therefore, distinguishes himself from the Lockean idea of disobeying and resisting a government only if it violates the rights of the citizens. However, what distinguishes Thoreau from the liberal tradition of political thought is that for him, the predicament is to democratize democracies, not to follow and obey them blindly. In this and other ways, Thoreau remains somewhat neither an anarchist nor a liberal, but a disobedient individual who abhors lethal acts of violence.

The central point of Thoreau's philosophy is that political harmony is no panacea, if indeed it is of any help at all in the struggle to reduce violence and injustice. As such, there is a 'higher law' than the law of the State. This is the law of moral conscience, what Socrates called his 'inner voice' (*daimon*). It is, therefore, the duty of the individual to obey her inner voice while disobeying the laws of the State. This is what Thoreau's humanist and nonviolent citizenship is about. For him, the law of morality precedes political expediency and, in such an event, the individual always has priority over the law of the State. As Thoreau notes: 'There will never be a really free and enlightened State. Until the State comes to recognize the individual as a higher and independent power, from which all its own power and authority are derived, and treats him accordingly.'[5] We can, thus, consider Thoreau's concept of civil disobedience as the revolt of the law of conscience, that of the inner voice, against the perversion of the political by the forces of government. What Thoreau suggests for us is to rethink through the idea of disobedience as a paradigm which holds out for a full and universal emancipation of the individual. But as Rudolf Rocker explains, Thoreau's 'so-called individualism was not the result of a negative attitude toward society but of a natural relation of man to man.'[6] Moreover, Thoreau gives us a radical view of freedom and citizenship, in which individuals are capable of creating themselves and the political world in which they live beyond all pre-defined boundaries. Last, but not least, the relevance of Thoreau's writings is due to the fact that he does not look at the State as an essential need in the happiness of modern man. As such, he starts his essay on *Civil Disobedience* with the famous dictum of Thomas Jefferson: 'That government is best which governs least', but he negates this phrase immediately by adding his own saying: 'That government is best which governs not at all.' Given Henry David Thoreau's moral attitude and his individualist intransigence, it comes not as a surprise to us to find him persuading citizens to return to the Socratic art of questioning, while asking them to serve their consciences before politics.

To be able to appreciate fully Thoreau's idea of disobedience, we need to be willing to examine as candidly as he did, the real nature of individual freedom as acts of self-actualization and self-organization. Here, we need to pause and to re-interpret democracy, not in terms of political expediency, where a citizen's supreme loyalty would be to a government, but in terms of a pattern of thinking, acting and relating to others, where citizens dare to affirm that as agents of freedom their loyalty is to the integrity of their minds. What calls for particular emphasis here is that as long as governments around the world deny the right of the individuals to be responsible for their moral and intellectual integrity and reject the art of disobeying and questioning as an act of subversion, the very notion of freedom as an ongoing self-invention and critical resistance against social and psychological repression is impossible.

That is to say, the basic definition of autonomy, as the outcome of a disobedient mind, applies to an individual who can freely decide on her guiding principles and ends. This redefinition of autonomy receives further force when, according to Cornelius Castoriadis, 'there is the effective possibility of the *choice of meaning* not dictated in advance.'[7] The question for Castoriadis is whether and how citizens in their practices of self-engagement and self-empowerment could step beyond the subjection to externally institutional laws. To set the stage, an autonomous democracy is a society that needs to educate self-reflective and self-reliant individuals, who have the psychological and social capacities to understand that social laws can be disobeyed because they are human creations. Society, thereby, becomes a space of active questioning and unlimited interrogation. In other words, collective self-governance and harmonious exchange among citizens go hand in hand, which Castoriadis calls 'to make, to do and to institute.'[8]

According to Castoriadis, 'Society does not halt before a conception, given once and for all, of what is just, equal or free, but rather institutes in such a way that the question of freedom, of justice, of equity and of equality might always be posed anew within the framework of the "normal" functioning of society.'[9] And this is precisely what creates the balance between the self-perpetuation and self-transformation of a disobedient mind and the active institution of society. In a nutshell, the idea of autonomy re-theorized and developed by Cornelius Castoriadis contrasts sharply with all forms of heteronomy (either religious or secular), which constrain the liberties of the subject to think and act differently and subversively. Similarly, the disobedient mind as an autonomous self assumes a blending of an inventive freedom and a creative praxis while standing for open-ended critical practices which diminish inequalities and indeterminations.

The creative impulses of the disobedient mind are, thus, deployed to criticize and reshape the inherited conceptions and processes of thinking through unconventional and marginal styles of reasoning and action. Following Castoriadis, we can say that in a disobedient mind, 'the construction of new "figures of the thinkable" is intimately bound up with "true interrogation", since the latter "implies the capacity to place in suspension the ultimate axioms, criteria and rules...with the supposition that others, not yet certain, perhaps not yet known, might replace them." The questioning of received notions "is paired with the positing of new forms/figures of the thinkable...unless one remains engaged in empty interrogation.".'[10]

Interestingly, creative reflection, as the outcome of a disobedient mind, may produce new ontological grounds for a new outlook on human beings and social life. That is why the disobedient mind very often occupies the centre stage in moving against all forms of established truth. Accordingly, the constant striving for freedom of the disobedient mind should also be seen as a permanent struggle against the residues of authoritarianism and inequality. This is a key lesson to be drawn from the life and action of Mahatma Gandhi as an Indian figure of self-rule and self-organization. Whatever grains of truth his arguments against conformism and conventional rationality may carry, his questioning of the principles of heteronomy in Indian society continues to have a greater echo at the very level of the hollow modes of living and controlled forms of liberty in our global world.

There is, in fact, a philosophical urgency to revisit Gandhi's interrogations in opposition and contradistinction to arguments and convictions advanced by our techno-capitalist global society that pretends to throw into doubt the two concepts of self-organization and self-institution of society. There are various reasons for leaning towards Gandhi in the present context. The overriding goal is to reflect on Gandhi as a thinker and practitioner of disobedience and autonomy, i.e. these unfettered expressions of the disobedient mind which assail static figures of our social being. As such, the focus on the ideas of Mahatma Gandhi makes sense on the grounds of his take on the Socratic art of questioning, as what he calls 'the acid test of reason', and his insistence on the concept of self-organizing and self-transforming democracy. Also, we need to point out that Gandhi's thought is singularly suited to the present problematic as an ontological and ethical commitment to individual autonomy. Gandhi's reflective engagements with fundamental assumptions of critical rationality display unique strengths and illuminating insights in relation with the modern concepts of freedom and autonomy.

Finally, this is what the French writer, George Bernanos, wrote in Brazil after escaping the Nazi occupation of France: 'I have thought for a long time now that if, some day, the increasing efficiency of the technique of destruction finally causes our species to disappear from the earth, it will not be cruelty that will be responsible for our extinction and still less, of course, the indignation that cruelty awakens and the reprisals and vengeance that it brings upon itself...but the docility, the lack of responsibility of the modern man, his base subservient acceptance of every common decree. The horrors which we have seen, the still greater horrors we shall presently see, are not signs that rebels, insubordinate, untameable men, are increasing in number throughout the world, but rather that there is a constant increase, a stupendously rapid increase, in the number of obedient, docile men.'[11]

PART I

DISOBEDIENCE
THROUGH THE AGES

1

A DISOBEDIENT MIND

In the long, storied tradition of disobedience through the ages, Gandhi stands tall as one of its pioneering practitioners on an Indian scale. Though his fame and his method of nonviolent dissent is well-known and practiced internationally, he remains after all a 'disobedient Indian'. It is practically impossible to live in India and not to see or hear references to Gandhi. He is by far the most recognizable Indian put on currency notes. He is also honoured all over the country with statues erected in the middle of town squares and his pictures posted on the walls of offices and shops, even restaurants. But this does not necessarily mean that Gandhi is well read and understood by all Indians. A quick look at everyday Indian politics and the debates in the press and elsewhere shows that the spirit of Gandhi is no longer fully present in his native country. Though his name is pronounced by all politicians and managers, when it comes to his teachings, young, middle-class technologists, corporate lawyers and businessmen in India consider Gandhi an old-fashioned figure, with his preference for an austere, simple lifestyle.

Despite being misread and misunderstood, Gandhi's legacy lives on, over seventy years after his death. Today, for many non-Indians, the name 'Gandhi' is synonymous with nonviolence and civil resistance. As such, Mahatma Gandhi continues to be studied and taken seriously by all those around the world, (including Indians) who are engaged in the struggle for freedom and democratization. Over the last seven decades, political and spiritual leaders and civil activists, from Martin Luther King Jr., Nelson Mandela, the Dalai Lama through to Abdallah Abu Rahmah, occasionally called the Palestinian Gandhi, from young militants of Otpor in Serbia to the freedom fighters of Tahrir Square in Egypt, have increasingly incorporated the Gandhian philosophy of resistance in their protest repertoires, realizing the ways in which it challenges the ruling elite's power and domination.

As such, the spirit of disobedient Gandhi, a heretic mind with a liberating power, has been like a torch which has enlightened generations of heretics who have followed his path. All those of us who are enjoying the freedoms of today and those of tomorrow, should take into our hearts the disobedience of Gandhi and those of all women and men who fought the battles of freedom for us and bought the prize of liberty with their genius, not with guns and prejudice. Let us not forget that any battle fought against fanatical intolerance and conformist thinking in the past seventy years after Gandhi's death has been in the name of a heretic Gandhi and not that of an ashramic Gandhi. Today, being like Gandhi is neither wearing khadi nor pretending to be an ashramic saint: it is simply having a disobedient mind. Gandhi had the simplicity of a great soul, but he also had the radicality of a heretic mind. If India remains a great nation, it is not because of its gurus, politicians, corporate leaders and Bollywood actors, but because it is the birthplace of a disobedient Indian, who gave rise to a new order of values and a new manner of mind. In truth, Gandhi's disobedient mind won him the proudest of destinies. He became a moment of the moral conscience of mankind.

Disobedience through the Ages

There were periods in which humankind felt her world to be meaningful and accommodated to the essence of life as she lived it. Today, however, though the human race regards itself as master of the world and has moulded the planet to its liking, the sense of realizing oneself, either as an individual or a society, has been lost. Therefore, we live a time when there is a major change in the ontological and political structures of human civilization, but there is also an increasing uncertainty and self-doubt about our beliefs concerning the aims of human civilization. In other words, being a global civilization is now a burden more than an asset in well-being. The promise of techno-science, as the last and only truth, has now turned into a dogmatic reasoning devoid of any philosophical meaning. Also, the crowding of human body and mind with the new communication technologies and the abundance of cheap and ugly skyscrapers and malls in the big cities around the world is accompanied by a strong and intense feeling of social hopelessness, existential loneliness and metaphysical boredom.

We could add to this another situation that previous generations could not foresee: that the turning of our contemporary civilization into decivilization is arriving with an unprecedented mixture of meaninglessness and thoughtlessness. Strangely enough, this thoughtlessness is presented to us as a blurred reality which we experience on an everyday basis and can hardly distinguish its degree of opacity from its level of clarity. This is perhaps because we neither believe in a God that can save us, nor do we expect to be saved by the intervention of a divine force. As such, we live in a world full of despair and devoid of promises. There are reasons to believe that the contemporary world, like the contemporary individual, is propelled by a process of thoughtlessness. As a result, we have entered a thought-provoking age where thoughtlessness has become the ordinary mode of living.

'The most thought-provoking thing about our thought-provoking age,' wrote Heidegger, 'is that we are still not thinking.'[12] What Heidegger calls 'thinking' is neither living an opinion, nor ratiocination. Thinking, Heidegger observes, is questioning. To think is to put the world and ourselves into question. As a matter of fact, only thinking that is involved in the practice of questioning is a way to creation *(poiesis)*. Therefore, if thinking *(noein)* has any validity as a concept and as a mode of being, it must mean that it is a protest against everything which is thoughtless. In view of this, as Heidegger affirms, only questioning is 'the unique habitat and locus of thinking.'[13] In other words, thinking is determined by a person who questions. It involves not only our receptivity to freedom but also the necessity to disobey. Therefore, it is only by asking questions that human beings can be an integral part of a common life and can realize their freedom. Each one of us must learn to do it for herself and, if possible, as a common project of autonomy. The call of thought is, thus, the call to freedom. But we come to understand what it means to be free when we ourselves can question and disobey a system. However, not everyone is capable of disobeying, just as not everyone is capable of thinking. According to Heidegger, 'We learn to think by giving our mind to what there is to think about.'[14] Such a process of learning will allow us to be delivered from the ugly spirit of complacency and conformity. Deliverance from conformity remains partly determined by what conformity itself is.

It should be immediately clear that in the real world people conform themselves to the opinion of others. This is a matter of self-silencing, As Cass R. Sunstein underlines in his book *Why Societies Need Dissent*, 'people silence themselves not because they believe they are wrong but because they do not want to face the disapproval that, they think, would follow from expressing the view they believe to be correct.'[15] By contrast, we could imagine a dissenter as a non-conformist who calls us into questioning. Moreover, dissent, even before dissenters, is at home with the prevalence of questioning as a manner of revealing the truth. If we understand the role of dissent, we will also see why it is so important to ensure disobedience as the unique mode of thinking. In considering this matter, it is not enough to say that thinking is only about disobeying unjust laws, for insofar as it can be defined, disobedience is a form of radical thinking which is both public and nonviolent. Furthermore, a disobedient mind involves not only disobedience of rules and laws, but it is mainly the critique and refusal of the legitimacy of an obligation to think in a certain way. Hence, all modes of thinking as disobedience are expressions of protest directed against the legitimacy of the established truth. That is the promise of a disobedient mind; it can help us to think about the world anew. So with a disobedient mind, the revolution of values should be no longer an exception; it should be the rule.

In many respects, the invention of the disobedient mind as a free and autonomous individual goes back to Socrates. Heidegger named Socrates 'the purest thinker of the West' because he practised thinking as the art of questioning. In the same line of thought, we can say that every critical reflection today, whether heretic or dissenting, gives birth, sometimes without knowing it, to the Socratic art of questioning. As such, we now know that even when rebellion is not completely realized, dissenting thinking preserves the power to protest against the thoughtlessness of society and the meaninglessness of life. The disobedient mind cannot turn away from the chaos of the world and the tragedy of history without denying the very principle of her disobedience. No one can consider the idea of freedom without the power of disobeying the unjust, the un-thought and the unfree. Albert Camus writes in *The Rebel* that 'Awareness, no matter how confused it may be, develops from every act of rebellion: the sudden, dazzling perception that there is something in man with which he can identify himself, even if only for a moment.'[16] The very moment that human beings refuse to obey the humiliating nature of heteronomy, they simultaneously proceed with the process of autonomy. With the disobedient mind, freedom is born. Two observations will support this affirmation. First, we can see that an act of thinking as questioning is not, essentially, a calculative act. Second, we can note that the idea of humanity is always present in this act of disobedience. As such, when we rebel against servility of mind, we do it in view of the nobility of spirit, but also in relation to the idea of human solidarity. This is because, as Karl Jaspers develops it brilliantly, 'Man is always something more than what he knows of himself. He is not what he is simply once for all, but is a process; he is not merely an extant life, but is, within that life, endowed with possibilities through the freedom he possesses to make of himself what he will by the activities on which he decides.'[17] In this light, freedom by definition is not only a political act, but also an ethical enterprise. In other words, freedom is more than a way of being; it is an art of becoming. Man is not what he is solely in virtue of his genetic code, but also, and much more, thanks to what education makes him. Education, therefore, is not only a process of nurturing the human soul, as the ancient Greeks understood it through the notion of *paideia*, meaning the acquisition and transmission of excellence, but also what philosopher Bertrand Russell defines as 'a certain outlook on life and the world.' The ancient Greeks understood *paideia* as the essence of culture and communication in a good society. The aim of *paideia*, Aristotle argues in *Politics*, is to enable members of a community to decide the political organization of society. Therefore, we need to assess the *paideic* dimensions of disobedience and freedom. This describes the ethical and spiritual foundations of the process of freedom building in or among societies. Education, as *paideia*, in virtue of its power of excellence, is the guarantor of the formation of a disobedient mind. This is no recipe for making mindless masses who do not really know what they want and are turned into irresponsible and conformist human armies that support populist regimes around the world.

In today's world, the rise of populist politicians across the globe signals a worrying trend of obedience, complacency and conformism among citizens of the world. What we can call the

'Trumpisation of politics', therefore, is not the cause of the erosion of public social trust and crisis of political action, but its severe symptom. A symptom which is pushing the zombified populations of America, the UK, Hungary, Turkey and elsewhere into bubbles of protectionism, nativism and exclusion. However, the most tragic part of the story is that the rise of mediocrity and complacency in contemporary political life is accompanied by a loss of dissenting minds among public intellectuals and the remaining gadflies of human civilization. As such, one of today's most important challenges lies in the act of questioning the reality of our world without necessarily taking it for granted. The act of questioning—as a Socratic gadfly and by a Socratic gadfly—is different from our habitual practices of asking questions, if any questions are asked. Any questioning which is truly public and transparent, addresses the challenges of its time. Hegel understood this well when in the preface to his *Elements of the Philosophy of Right*, he wrote: 'Philosophy is its own time apprehended in thoughts.' In other words, the philosophical formation of a public gadfly is itself based on a marginal and non-institutional approach to the question of critical engagement. Therefore, to practice dissent today as a public gadfly is not only to practice what Edward Said called 'speaking truth to power' but more precisely to live and think outside the mental ghettos of our societies as a constructive marginal. It is only by being a dissenting outsider that one can radically rethink the very basic foundations of our common humanity and its corruption into a decivilizing process.

The relevant question, therefore, is not why we are dissenting, but what we can do with our dissent. Not surprisingly, the simple act of non-conforming could be an expression of dissent. Here, there is not only a call for the renewal of social questioning, but also a way of remaining true to the ethical through an effort of exemplarity. It is, thus, only by being exemplar, that is, living and thinking against the current, that a public gadfly can leave a sustainable influence on the public scene. That is why, dissent, more than being a simple manner of protesting, is an invitation to awareness.

Through its art of questioning, the real task of dissent is to challenge and defeat the twin corruptions of democracy: Imposed conformism and normalized complacency. And also because democracy is about questioning and dissenting, to be a guardian of the democratic soul is not to give one's allegiance to those with whom we are embedded as a community of citizens. That is why any allegiance to democracy should not turn imperatively into an allegiance to the politicians and the principles of the State. In the same way, any allegiance to academy is not a form of servility to the suggestions of the Vice Chancellor or Registrar of a university. In that sense, good citizenship is not separable from the exercise of the right to question one's consent with regard to an institution. It is only such public consciousness which shapes a republic of gadflies. Now, however, it is rare to find self-awareness and self-criticism among the intellectual conditions of present-day politics. This, in itself, shows the difficult task of public gadflies, who need to grow up culturally and mature politically outside of, and in opposition to, the hermetic structures of our civilization. Perhaps one should add that Socratic gadflies have always been and will continue to be disturbers of unquestioned power and non-democratic consensus. As Vaclav Havel affirms: 'The intellectual should constantly disturb, should bear witness to the misery of the world, should be provocative by being independent, should rebel against all hidden and open pressure and manipulations, should be the chief doubter of systems, of power and its incantations, should be a witness to their mendacity.'[18]

Truly speaking, the quality and character of moral and political leadership, which is committed to dialogue and inclusion, is related to the nature of dissent in our contemporary societies.

However, if this is not case, as in the case of the process of 'Trumpisation of politics', disquieting thoughtlessness and fanatic self-assertiveness would take over. In such an unexamined political life, the dynamic of living together turns into an aimless and meaningless activity. Gadflies, therefore, have the philosophical task and the political responsibility of exposing the shortcomings of their own political society and its institutions with sincerity and critical mindedness.

But the greatest moral strength of a Socratic gadfly is his moral capital. Moral capital does not connote merely being ethical in politics or having feelings of empathy for the sufferings and misfortunes of others. The moral capital of a public gadfly is to grapple with the ethical problem of the use of violence in the face of the political evil. The key point here is that, whatever the critical approach of a Socratic gadfly in regard to an unjust or mediocre social system which needs to be transformed, the quest is pursued in accordance with, and not to the detriment of, compassionate solidarity. As Martin Luther King Jr. remarks, 'that one seeks to defeat the unjust system, rather than individuals who are caught in that system. And that one goes on believing that somehow this is the important thing, to get rid of the evil system and not the individual who happens to be misguided, who happens to be misled, who was taught wrong. The thing to do is to get rid of the system and thereby create a moral balance within society.'[19] In the light of this moral and intellectual urgency, it is plausible to conclude that in the age of the 'Trumpisation of politics' the only way to respond to the blows of fate is not to lose the appetite for dissent and critical thinking and not cease to ask embarrassing questions. As Jean-Paul Sartre says: 'The intellectual is someone who meddles with what does not concern him.' That is why, to practice dissent in an age of Trump is to have dirty hands, because thinking must position itself in relation to politics. For thinking and questioning are neither public agreements nor business contracts. They are constitutive for all public action and political organization of the society. If humankind is looking towards a future, it necessarily requires convictions and commitments, but it also requires Socratic rebels, of the mind and of action, who have the courage to swim against the tide and think against the general drift to superfluity and meaninglessness.

The disobedient mind creates a new grammar for itself in philosophy, art and politics. This grammar is based on a 'breakthrough' from the passivity of the perpetually renewed sameness. This breakthrough, however, far from being an intellectualist faith, is nothing more than a critical mode of cognition confronted with questions concerning the inexorable course of human destiny. No definite or convincing answer can be given to the question: 'How should we construct our freedom?' But what we know is that such a question is not a given, but a task. As Jaspers says, 'Man, living man, will answer this question through his own being, in the course of his own activities.'[20] We can see how this absence of mental fatalism could be driven to a self-consciousness (in the Hegelian sense of the term) where livelihood itself turns into an enterprise of freedom. The concept of freedom is indeed a key notion in the Hegelian philosophical system. Hegel believed that it is also the central concept in human history. 'Mind is free,' he wrote, 'and to actualise this, its essence—to achieve this excellence—is the endeavour of the world-mind in world-history.'

For Hegel, 'to be free is to be at home with oneself (*bei sich*) in what is the other'. It is, therefore, essential to the freedom of the self that its thought and action can be related to the freedom of the other. Our mind should, thus, be attuned to the process of life as becoming free. That is to say, Hegel's concept of freedom is neither static nor lifeless. It then becomes evident that thinking in Hegelian terms is a lively movement from Being to Becoming. For Hegel, Being as self-consciousness is set in motion by self-consciousness. In other words, Hegel believes that 'every item of knowledge altered the knower; being the altered, he must seek in his world a new knowledge of himself; in this way the stream flowed on unrestingly, for being and consciousness of being were severed, and they must perpetually renew their severance in a changed form, passing from one to the other; such was and is man's historical process.'[21] Thinking in terms of Hegelian philosophy of freedom, one can say that the disobedient mind is the unrestful moment of man's self-consciousness. It follows from this that the crisis of self-existence as autonomy is related to man's indifference to himself and to the world.

As Erich Fromm affirms in his book *Man for Himself*: 'We have lost the sense of significance and uniqueness of the individual, that we have made ourselves into instruments for purposes outside ourselves, that we experience and treat ourselves as commodities, and that our own powers have become alienated from ourselves. We have become things and our neighbours have become things. The result is that we feel powerless and despise ourselves for our impotence.'[22] The herd mentality underlined by Fromm can be described as a dark situation in which humankind lacks the courage of thinking independently while not daring to trust his own judgment. As such, if freedom, as the ability to preserve one's being, has a meaning, it rests upon the fulfillment of one's nobility of mind in the Spinozist sense of the term. 'Preserving one's being means to Spinoza to become that which one potentially is... (Therefore) Spinoza is radically opposed to authoritarian ethics. To him man is an end-in-himself and not a means for an authority transcending him.'[23] In order to fulfill his end, man needs to listen to his inner voice, as an expression of his conscience, against any form of obedience. However, as Fromm puts it, 'listening to oneself is so difficult because this art requires another ability, rare in modern man: that of being alone with oneself.'[24] As a result, a disobedient man does not fear to be alone with himself, for the good reason, that he listens to himself without being frightened at the prospect of facing himself.

Heidegger also honours listening in his own way when talking about thinking. For him, there is no learning without listening. 'What we can do in our present case,' writes Heidegger, 'or anyway can learn, is to listen closely. To learn listening, too, is the common concern of student and teacher. No one is to be blamed, then, if he is not yet capable of listening. But by the same token you must concede that the teacher's attempt may go wrong and that, where he happens not to go wrong, he must often resign himself to the fact that he cannot lay before you in each instance all that should be stated.'[25]

The point Heidegger tries to make is to show us the intimate connection between thinking and learning to think. His reference to Socrates as a teacher bears witness to his first and foremost preoccupation with the craft of educating the students. Furthermore, Heidegger guides us in the matter of thinking, to the art of education. Going back to Spinoza's concept of 'potency' (*potentia*), we can add hereby that education is no more than helping a human being realize her potentiality. This is one of the main conditions of a disobedient mind which learns how to think and how to question reality. That is why, as Fromm underlines, 'the opposite of education is manipulation, which is based on the absence of faith in the growth of potentialities...'[26]

There is no need for faith in an obedient mind, a mind which does not question reality, since there is no potentiality for autonomy in it either. The call of thought is thus the call to clear a way for oneself out of the conditions of conformity and manipulation. It is a process of unmoulding oneself. Only an education truly involved with critical thinking and the Socratic art of questioning can help individuals to rest upon their ability to take a life in excellence and exemplarity seriously. 'But if education is once more to become what it was in its best days, namely the possibility, through historical continuity, of developing into a human being possessed of full selfhood, that can only ensue through a faith which, amid all necessary strictness in learning and practice, indirectly conveys a spiritual value.'[27]

If, as Jaspers explains, man cannot live and learn without a spiritual value, then the crucial question for our century and the next ones is whether man's inclination to power and violence could be considered as an integral part of his spirituality. It follows from the standpoint of a disobedient mind that disobedience is neither a taste for power nor a passion to destroy. This could not have been possible if the dogma of man's innate natural destructiveness were true. Indeed, to think like Socrates, the real source of evilness would be nothing but ignorance. Meister Eckhart expresses this idea beautifully in his *Fragments*: 'That I am a man, this I share with other men. That I see and hear and that I eat and drink is what all animals do likewise. But that I am I is only mine and belongs to me and to nobody else; to no other man not to an angel nor to God...'[28]

In other words, the disobedient mind is alone, but it is related and interconnected at the same time. As such, man's political nature depends on the harmony and the exchange he has with his fellow men. Thus, the political defines the nature of being human and the more political we are, the more human we are. The political is inherent in man as a being-in-the-world. Hence, learning to act politically is as much a discovery of our own nature as human beings as it is a discovery of the nature of the world. Yet, the relatedness and interconnectedness of human beings to each other and to the world is so integral that consideration of one involves the investigation of the other. However, though we act in the world to express our freedom as human beings, we first grasp the world by asking questions about it. In other words, it is as political actors that we think the world and we put it into question. It is through this process of questioning that we accept the responsibility of disobeying certainties in order to give meaning to our lives. Because, there is no meaning to life except the meaning we give to it by living disobediently. We repeat then, that understanding of man's political situatedness in the world must proceed from the understanding of his capacity to transcend and transform laws, rules and institutions in the name of his capacities for self-questioning and self-creation.

2

QUESTIONING THE POLITICAL

Man is 'zoon politikon' (ζωον πολιτικον), a political animal, wrote Aristotle nearly 2,400 years ago. Yet, twenty centuries later, Kant made reference to the 'unsocial sociability' of human beings in the Fourth Thesis of his *Idea for a Universal History from a Cosmopolitan Point of View*. In other words, there are limits to what human beings can do as political animals. Therefore, though human beings can act in common, they also need to learn to live and create politically together.

That is to say, without a sense of the political, mankind descends into disorder, chaos and barbarity. However, what history teaches us is that human beings are neither good or bad, nor just or unjust by nature. There is no such thing as 'radical evil' in history per se, if it is not being created by the work of human beings. As Voltaire says majestically,

'Those who can make you believe absurdities, can make you commit atrocities.' Human beings, therefore, can politically create the radical evil, as they can socially promote injustice. In other words, humankind kills and justifies murder for political reasons. The end of laws and institutions, thus, is to prevent or promote murder and mass killings. But, though the political presupposes discord and dissent, it does not suggest, however, the insoluble war of all against all. That is why the political is the nonviolent management of all conflicts. The political, thus, starts where the violence ends. What we face here is not the question of the practicality of ethics, but that of the limits of the political. But talking about the limits of the political does not necessarily mean pointing to its end. For the good reason that the end of the political is the end of history, and more precisely the end of all human struggle for liberty.

As a matter of fact, the human struggle for liberty is the principle of action of the political. For, as Hannah Arendt points out correctly, it is 'the world of relationships that arises out of action— man's essential political activity...'[29] Because most of our experience with the political is expressed on the grounds of politics, it is, therefore, necessary to distinguish between the two concepts of the 'political' and 'politics'.

Every questioning about the essence of the political, as the art of organizing a society, is *a fortiori* a questioning on the meaning of politics as the space of interaction between conflicting powers which try to govern the society. As such, the political is the space of autonomous action of human beings in a historical context, while politics is the space of competition and contestation for the very basis of power and authority. Politics, so we are told, is understood as a strategy for governing humans as social beings. Equally as old as politics is the political, which has also existed in all times and among human beings, as the public sense of living together. As Hannah Arendt underlines, 'Because man is not self-sufficient but is dependent in his existence on others, provisions must be made that affect the existence of all, since without such provisions, communal life would be impossible.'[30]

In other words, the role of the political is to safeguard the communal existence of the individuals, or more precisely to preserve and promote exchange and harmony in a human society. The Aristotelian definition of 'man as a political animal' is applied to the organization of the *polis* rather than to human beings' ability to rule and govern other individuals. Moreover, the activity of living together precedes that of mastering others. In this sense, the political is understood as not being dominated or dominating, but as a public construct that guarantees the exercise of freedom of individuals. But in order to be free in the space of the political, individuals need to be freed from politics as the space of domination. The Athenians understood the *agora*, the marketplace, as the crucial space for freedom. Dialogue, as the end result of *agora*, established limits to the realm of the political. In a sense, the Athenians, and mostly Socrates, knew well that where there is a possibility of dialogue, there is absence of violence. However, what was known to Athenians as a frontier between dialogue, as the possibility of speech, and violence, as the silencing of speech, was unable to arrest the historical degradation of the political, as the realm of living and speaking together, into politics as a space of domination of the others.

The political is never acquired and fashioned in solitude, and also never where human beings come together as masses and not as citizens. Thus while each work of politics is a unique whole presented to the political in finalized form, the political itself is an ongoing reality, in need of exchange among citizens and mutual re-evaluation and transformation, in view of its essence. Yet when we look at history, the experience of the political has always remained brief and temporary. Most human beings are in need of the political, in order to express their hope in being free, but it is always a limited minority among humanity, who are able to devote extensive periods of their heart and mind to it. Thus, we continue to live off the fruits of the political. The political remains the continuous reality of our transformative life, but it is always accompanied by the eternal human desire for domination and conquest. Reformulating this desire in terms of the Hegelian philosophy, Albert Camus writes in *The Rebel*, 'The entire history of mankind is, in any case, nothing but a prolonged fight to the death for the conquest of universal prestige and absolute power.'[31]

The political brings us together, where politics divide us. As such, though not a disinterested act, the political is always collective and in a spirit of solidarity. Solidarity is a reciprocated sense of empathy and a consciousness in the commitments of others to shared purposes. It is the affirmation of the dignity of each person in a relation of harmonic exchange. Solidarity exists in solidary obligations, also called obligations *in solido*. As such, individual commitment to the harmonization of the society is the highest form of self-interest for a person who is engaged in a political exchange with the others. If the political is the goal in organizing the society, solidaristic exchange is certainly the path we are meant to walk. Unlike politics, which is always enclosed in a certain ideological or idealistic framework, the political keeps leading the citizens down new paths and opening new doors. These transformative paths turn egoistic individuals into conscious and committed citizens who have the capacity to act and to create collectively. Citizens who are engaged with the task of the political no longer expect miraculous social changes either from revolutions or from the market economy. While in quest of questioning, they refuse to surrender their souls to the prophets of apocalypse and the heralds of false happiness.

As a matter of fact, in the domain of the political, happiness is a stranger, and when it intrudes upon our political exchange, freedom is lost. We have only to remind ourselves that it lies in the nature of the political to deal with social harmony and not with love and to be loved. As Hannah Arendt says, 'People who become organized have in common what are ordinarily called interests. The directly personal relationship, where one can speak of love, exists of course foremost in real love, and it also exists in a certain sense in friendship. There a person is addressed directly, independent of his relation to the world. Thus, people of the most divergent organizations can still be personal friends. But if you confuse these things, if you bring love to the negotiating table, to put it bluntly, I find that fatal.'[32] What Arendt portrays and analyzes as the public space, is a place for the exchange of political interests and actions, where citizens reveal themselves to others. In other words, Arendt describes the realm of the political as a world stage that channels and defines important aspects of what makes us human. This emphasis on the political as a transformative sphere, where individuals have to communicate and exchange their interests into that which is common to all, is a way of stepping out of the egoistic self of the personal and private domain. Not surprisingly, for Arendt the most valuable human mode of living is action. Because, as she proclaims in *Between Past and Future*, 'Men are free [...] as long as they act, neither before nor after; for to be free and to act are the same.'[33]

The essence of humanity, therefore, is to be engaged in political action and not only to be an *animal laborans* or a *homo faber*. Unlike what social Darwinism would like to make us believe, all aspects of the human condition are related to the political dimension of human beings and not necessarily to the maintenance of the biological survival of mankind. Therefore, human beings essentially belong to two orders of existence: the biological and the political. But what is imposed upon us by the needs of political life (*bios politikos*) is in sharp distinction from the biological condition of human beings. It must be admitted that the human capacity for the political is in exact opposition to our natural inclinations. 'According to Greek thought, the human capacity for political organization is not only different from but stands in direct opposition to that natural association whose center is the home (*oikia*) and the family...Of all the activities necessary and present in human communities, only two were deemed to be political and to constitute what Aristotle called the *bios politikos*, namely action (*praxis*) and speech (*lexis*)...'[34]

The Greeks knew well that the political is contrary to the cosmological and the biological views of the world and humankind. That is why they considered the political realm as an infinitely desacralized communal space (*koinonia*). All this presupposed a profound change in their view of the world and of human beings. This paradigm shift was based on a new definition of the human being as an animal capable of speaking and acting in relationship to others, rather than a simple fabricator of tools and things of the world. Perhaps we can best measure the gulf between the *homo faber* and the *homo politikos* if we recall that the universal harmonious order thought and developed by Aristotle was accompanied by an effort of secularization and rationalization of the divine cosmological harmony of Hesiod in his *Theogony*, describing the origins and genealogies of the Greek gods. Hesiod considers the cosmos as being divine

and logical (*theion* and *logos*), therefore made
by the gods and understood by human beings. In
Hesiod, the world emerges from the groundlessness
and the emptiness. Hesiod's universe is, therefore,
underpinned by chaos and permeated by disorder,
but human beings are inspired by the Muses in
the artistic creation and the pursuit of knowledge.
That is to say, Hesiod was very much concerned
with moral and practical issues of life. Therein lay
the great importance of the myths for the ancient
Greeks. 'The Greeks used their myths to attempt
to make sense of all the disorder around them,
to put order where there was none, and by doing
so, justified the way the gods treated them. And
the myths helped to explain why their world was
the way it was.'[35] Out of Hesiod's cosmological
view of a harmonious world came a philosophical
representation of the world. It was the exigency
of a rational argumentation that distinguished the
mythological perception of the world (*mythos)*
from a rational questioning of the world *(logos)*.
The radicality of this questioning among the
Greek philosophers made a break for the rise of
democracy in Athens. This is where one needs to
be more careful with the notion of 'the political'.
According to Cornelius Castoriadis, 'The Greeks
did not invent "the" political, in the sense of the
dimension of explicit power always present in any

society. They invented—or, better, created—politics, which is something entirely different.... Politics, such as it was created by the Greeks, amounts to the explicit putting into question of the established institution of society. This presupposes that at least important parts of this institution had nothing "sacred" or "natural" about them, but rather that they represented *nomos*.'[36] What Castoriadis is referring to hereby is an ongoing movement of the questioning of the established institution of society. Political philosophy, therefore, is from the very beginning a truly radical way of questioning the political. In other words, 'The creation of democracy and philosophy is truly the creation of historical movement in the strong sense—a movement which, in this phase, deploys itself from the eighth to the fifth century, and is, in fact, brought to an end with the defeat of Athens in 404 [BCE].'[37] What the Greeks discovered (which was lost later with the institution of theological politics) was the idea of non-sacredness of the *nomos* and the historical revolution of the idea of *paideia*. Thus, 'it is no accident that the renewal of political thought in Western Europe is quickly accompanied by the resurgence of radical "utopias". These utopias manifest, first and foremost, awareness of this fundamental fact: institutions are human works. And it is no accident either that, contrary to the poverty, in this respect, of contemporary "political philosophy," grand political philosophy from Plato to Rousseau has placed the question of *paideia* at the center of its interests. Even if, practically considered, the question of education has always remained a concern of modern times, this great tradition dies, in fact, with the French Revolution.'[38] The Athenian *paideia* did not represent a simple form of social education, but it marked a pattern of life for the male citizens of Athens. That is why Pericles in his funeral oration attributes Athens' greatness to the *Weltanschauung* of the Athenians. As we read in *The History of the Peloponnesian War*, written by Thucydides in 431 BCE, Pericles describes the Athenians in the following words:

> Our constitution does not copy the laws of neighbouring states; we are rather a pattern to others than imitators ourselves. Its administration favours the many instead of the few; this is why it is called a democracy. If we look to the laws, they afford equal justice to all in their private differences; if no social standing, advancement in public life falls to reputation for capacity, class considerations not being allowed to interfere with merit; nor again does poverty bar the way, if a man is able to serve the state, he is not hindered by the obscurity of his condition. The freedom which we enjoy in our government extends also

to our ordinary life. There, far from exercising a jealous surveillance over each other, we do not feel called upon to be angry with our neighbour for doing what he likes, or even to indulge in those injurious looks which cannot fail to be offensive, although they inflict no positive penalty. But all this ease in our private relations does not make us lawless as citizens. Against this fear is our chief safeguard, teaching us to obey the magistrates and the laws, particularly such as regard the protection of the injured, whether they are actually on the statute book, or belong to that code which, although unwritten, yet cannot be broken without acknowledged disgrace.[39]

What the funeral oration of Pericles shows us is that the purpose of *paideia* as civic education was largely considered to aid the individuals in their movement to achieve *arête,* or moral excellence. However, the great Athenian philosopher, Socrates, extended the meaning of *paideia* to include not only *vita activa* but also *vita contemplativa.* As such, Socrates as we know him through Plato's *Dialogues*, placed a great value on the education of the mind and promotion of harmony. Though Socrates testifies in Plato's *Apology* (31d) that he stayed out of party politics because factional politics would have been the end of his contemplative life, he, nonetheless, provides us with a valuable account of his method of *elenchus,* or cross-examination, as an art of questioning politics and politicians. The Socratic ideal of committed questioning can be seen as an effort to combine the practice of philosophy with the Athenian tradition of democracy. 'We must, of course, recognize that the Athenian democratic order practiced—and celebrated—gender inequality, xenophobia, imperialism, and slavery. But doing so does not require us to deny that the idea and practice of democracy was an invention of the Greek polis. It was at this historical moment that there emerged both the idea that all citizens, regardless of differences of wealth, birth, talents, trade, or profession, should be political equals and a stable set of practices that effectively placed power in the hands of the common (non-elite) mass of citizens.'[40] What the ancient Greeks remind us is that the striving for individual and social harmony depends on the balance between the individual quest for *arête*, or moral excellence, and the shared conceptions of solidarity and community service. As such, the Athenian political life of the marketplace and the social arena of competing interests had nothing to do with our modern conception of politics limited by the vocabularies of utilitarianism, egoistic individualism and mass technology.

With the Romans, the concept of the political turned into that of 'imperium', the power to command. The Romans were different from the Greeks in the sense that they attributed a sacred foundation to the power and authority of Rome. Rome was the universal and eternal city, *Urbs, ab urbe condita*. Though historians have dismissed the story of Romulus and Remus as a legend, the Romans considered Rome as an intrinsically urban and political sacred space. This sacred space, by the Latin name of *Pomerium (post-moerium*: behind the wall), was dedicated to the gods in gratitude for their protection of the city of Rome. Assuredly, because Rome was considered as a universal city, being a Roman citizen was a privileged political and legal status. *Civitas* was acquired by birth if both parents were Roman *cives*. This was also a rule in ancient Athens, but unlike the Athenians, the Romans attributed too much power and privilege to the generals and emperors, who could grant citizenship to non-Romans. But what was special about the Romans, which was later inherited by the moderns, is the importance of the law. As such, the degree to which the political space, as the body of the citizens, was valued and sustained in the Roman republic was directly related to the body of the law. It was the law that brought the citizens together and created a *res publica*. However, while the laws of Athens appealed to the concept of *nomos* as a social contract made among Athenians, the Romans developed the idea of 'natural', which afforded a clear sacredness to its origin. 'The sanctity of natural law, which Cicero seems to insist on, is granted by the sacredness of blood relations, which natural law regulates. Moreover, by emphasizing the sanctity of natural law, Cicero seems to openly recall the theological and ethical interpretation of the laws of nature, and also of natural law.'[41] This legal arrangement in the Roman world closed the doors on the Athenian grasp of the political as a new grasp of the world as self-creation and provided a strong philosophical and legal platform for the future instituted heteronomy of early Christianity.

The Roman empire, in comparison to ancient Athens, is already a heteronomous society, but with the Christian world we enter a new phase of the political in the ancient world, where we are confronted explicitly with the inability of a human society to recognize itself as the creator of its own laws and institutions. Cornelius Castoriadis calls this type of society a *heteronomous* society, in contrast to the *autonomous* society, where the self-institution of the political is a perpetual process of citizens' struggle for freedom. However, 'Arendt claims that freedom for the Romans was not "an attribute of the will but an accessory of doing and acting."'[42] This is, most probably, the huge difference that exists between the Roman society, a society of *auctoritas* and *imperium*, with the early Christian society, which is fundamentally a gift of the Holy Spirit.

Accordingly, the Holy Spirit is called the Spirit of sanctity (*Spiritus Sanctus*). That is why 'Hannah Arendt attributes to Christianity the idea that the essential human freedom is freedom of the individual will.'[43] Saint Augustine and later Saint Thomas Aquinas re-arrange Plato's allegory of the Cave in *The Republic*, where Plato represents the public world in terms of shadows and darkness, and suggests the metaphysical priority of *theôria* over *praxis*. Therefore, the realm of the political is subordinated to the *bios theôretikos* and becomes instrumental for the ends of the world of Ideas. With St Augustine, we have the epistemological inversion of the concept of the political, as the realm of human affairs where the two questions of freedom and justice are discussed, to *De civitate Dei*, the City of God, as the perfect political society. In other words, for Augustine, 'Political history is governed by God's providence. To the extent that historical explanations are possible, they must refer to it [...] He therefore uses the City of God as a standard against which actual political societies, especially the great empires, can be measured and found wanting. This enables Augustine to expose the vanity of their moral pretensions and to heighten his readers' desire to be members of that city where the "Supreme Good is to be found".'[44]

As we can see, the Augustinian theologization of the politics depoliticizes the political and takes its true essence out of the public space. Unlike the Greek *polis*, the theological-political does not stand for the space of appearance, but as a private space of conscience. In Greece, as Castoriadis says, 'religion is kept strictly at bay by political activities.'[45] That is to say, where there is no indeterminate freedom of creative imagination and no possibility of questioning religion, the question of the political, as the space of togetherness and interconnectedness, is pushed to the second level of importance. Let us not forget that politics is not the will of God, but the action of human beings. It is, therefore, limited and uncertain. As Arendt puts it, 'Wherever people gather together, it is potentially there, but only potentially, not necessarily and not forever.'[46] Thus, the space of the political becomes the fragile space of human exchange, where the two conceptions of freedom and individuation are intimately related. The body political of a people is not a realm of transcendence, but that of transformation. Therefore, the *zoon politikon* is defined as a creature that has the capacity to act, to exchange and to transform. The capacity to think in terms of exchange and transformation is a political ability that enables individuals to orient themselves in the openness of the public sphere and to judge and choose the realm of the political. This political capacity of judging and choosing openly and freely is absent from the monolithic logic of the theologico-political. As Castoriadis says: 'this activity of judging and choosing, and the very idea of it, is a Greco-Western activity and idea—it has been created in this world and nowhere else. The idea would not and could not occur to a Hindu, to a classical Hebrew, to a true Christian or to a Muslim. Classical Hebrews have nothing to choose. They have been given the truth and the Law once and for all by God, and if they started judging and choosing about that they would no longer be Hebrew. Likewise, true Christians have nothing to judge or choose: they have to believe and to love. For, it is written: *Judge not, that ye be not judged* (Matt. 7:1).'[47]

What Castoriadis tries to develop here is the relation between the political realm of self-questioning, as practiced in ancient Athens, and the complex exposition of autonomy. Unlike the religious societies which are heteronomous, there is no truth in an autonomous society that we must logically question our way to: there are many truths, and they all extend well beyond the imposed limits of the theological-political. The seeds of autonomy which had already been sown by Pericles—or really by the Athenian vison of the political—were passed on in artistic and philosophical terms to the painters of the Renaissance like Michelangelo and Leonardo and to the writers and thinkers of eighteenth-century Europe like Diderot, Montesquieu, Rousseau and Voltaire. In terms of praxis, the two great revolutions of the eighteenth century, the American Revolution and the French Revolution, were not only the products of the ideals of the Enlightenment, but mainly two periods of realization of social and political autonomy. According to Castoriadis, the spirit of *autonomy*, which disappears with the decline of the Athenian *polis*, comes into being again during the American Revolution in the Town Hall meetings and later, in the French Revolution and in the local assemblies of the Paris Commune. The notion of autonomy can be found here in the spontaneous 'acting in concert' that characterizes the rise of the political against instituted politics.

As it was mentioned previously, one central characteristic of the 'political' is the questioning *of* and *in* the public realm. But we need to add to this the communicative and transformative aspects of the political impulse. As both Arendt and Castoriadis show us in their writings, failing to distinguish between *politics*, as regulation and representation of power, and *political*, as open, imaginative and spontaneous discussion, deliberation and action in the public sphere, comes to cover up the radical potential of creativity and transformation of human beings. As such, the objective of the political is not the well-being of the people, but the ability and the quality of living together and antagonizing one another. Chantal Mouffe, in her inspiring work entitled *On the Political* defines 'politics' as 'the set of practices and institutions through which an order is created,' while she understands 'the political' as 'the dimension of antagonism'.[48] A key point of Mouffe's approach is that, by drawing a lesson from the work of Carl Schmitt, it challenges the liberal political discourse of compromise, tolerance and human sociability. As such, Mouffe negates the idea of non-adversarial democracy, while putting into question 'the unchallenged hegemony of neoliberalism with its claim that there is no alternative to the existing order.'[49] The danger pinpointed by Mouffe is that political confrontation in a democratic context is replaced by an illusory form of social organization and democratic legitimation which is neither argumentative nor deliberative, but sadly, consensual and majoritarian. What this ontological change of this adversarial political into demonizing and moralizing politics reveals, is how the sense of privatization of the individual and the anti-political element prevalent in liberal politics, as in the totalitarian regime, is not conducive to the establishment of a public space beyond the conformist dynamics of political parties in today's world.

The question we need to ask is whether the anti-political feature of politics in today's world has put an end to the questioning of the political itself, disabling us to comprehend what Alexis de Tocqueville saw as the inherent contradictions of democracy. According to the French political philosopher, Claude Lefort, 'Tocqueville's idea that democratic freedom can be transformed into servitude still survives in our day.' In other words, 'If Tocqueville is to be believed, the individual either appears in the fullness of his self-affirmation, or disappears completely as a result of his weakness and isolation, and is swallowed up by opinion or social power.'[50] What Lefort is referring to here is the idea of the political lost in the massification of politics. The overtaking of the political by contemporary crowds, both in the totalitarian and democratic contexts goes hand in hand with the loss of the instinctive reflexes for freedom and the rise of what we call the 'lumpenpolitics'. We, therefore, find once again that the divorce between a democratic passion Athenian style and the Constantian idea of 'enjoyment of private rights' (*jouissances privees*) creates more and more of a gap between the private realm and the public realm. It appears to us that in contemporary politics, the large gap created between the public and the private has torn apart the tissue of the political. To understand this, we can turn once to Tocqueville and his *Democracy in America*:

> Subjection in minor affairs breaks out every day and is felt by the whole community indiscriminately. It does not drive men to resistance, but it crosses them at every turn, till they are led to surrender the exercise of their own will. Thus their spirit is gradually broken and their character enervated; whereas that obedience which is exacted on a few important but rare occasions only exhibits servitude at certain intervals and throws the burden of it upon a small number of men. It is in vain to summon a people who have been rendered so dependent on the central power to choose from time to time the representatives of that power; this rare and brief exercise of their free choice, however important it may be, will not prevent them from gradually losing the faculties of thinking, feeling, and acting for themselves, and thus gradually falling below the level of humanity.[51]

Tocqueville's argument implies a wider problematic, that of freedom, which highlights another blind spot of contemporary politics. This is to say, that different strands of liberal thought, exemplified by a process of forging a range of value-choices and individual options, suffer extremely from the absence of a sense of autonomy and self-creation. Hence, contemporary liberal theories reformulate the concept of freedom in terms of negative liberty without focusing necessarily on a fuller account of freedom as self-questioning, self-invention and self-determination. As a result, citizens are safeguarded from illiberal forms of interference by a system of rights, but they do not feel the urge of participating in an unregulated public space where we can find a confrontation of ideas. As a result, the process of freedom is defined by the State and the citizens as a way to display all the virtues of individual rights by supporting social institutions, and not as a mode of setting one's social and political action in an autonomous and critical manner which encourages self-institution and questioning of the status quo. The state of affairs, therefore, is echoed vibrantly by a sense of fear, insecurity and uncertainty about the real possibilities of the political. Such a sense of political impotency given to us by the global prominence of meaninglessness does not facilitate a reflective engagement with the fundamental assumptions of politics in today's world. As such, the general disbelief about the creative and emancipative capacities and capabilities of human beings have turned into a habit of unlimited acceptance of nonsensical junk thought. The monological character of this junk thought goes hand in hand with the very idea of the institutionalization of un-doubt. This reign of un-doubt in contemporary society is where no claims to truth come under suspicion with respect to their ontological grounds and socio-political side effects. This has become a standard definition of human essence in a meaningless world of liberal conformism. This argument presumes, therefore, that a critical take on democratic thought and action can fuel a keener perception and analysis of a citizen ethos that fosters an imaginative agonism against all forms of complacency and conservatism.

3

THE UNHOLY CROWDS:
DOCILITY AND OBEDIENCE

Modern politics has always been aware of its inner evil and therefore has tried to dissimulate it. As such, it deceives everyone at all times. That is the reason why, even when politics is not a system of domination, it is a conscious process of lying and demagogy *a necessitate*. The desire to turn citizens into unquestioning, unaccountable and servile human beings has become the principal motive for the development of politics in the contemporary world. According to Wilhelm Reich, 'What has to be explained is not the fact that the man who is hungry steals or the fact that the man who is exploited strikes, but why the majority of those who are hungry don't steal and why the majority of those who are exploited don't strike.'[52] Reich's question has never been so pertinent as it is in our world today. That the many are ruled by the few, is a historical fact in every culture. Nevertheless, the question of servility and submission of human beings to norms and institutions that constrain their freedom remains a startling point that demonstrates the process of degradation of the political. This point was well understood and discussed by Etienne de la Boétie, in his famous pamphlet, *De La Servitude Volontaire*, where he goes on to make a case as to why people submit their consent to tyrants and why they ought to withdraw their consent immediately. 'Shall we call subjection to such a leader cowardice?' wrote de la Boétie:

> 'Shall we say that those who serve him are cowardly and faint-hearted? If two, if three, if four, do not defend themselves from the one, we might call that circumstance surprising but nevertheless conceivable. In such a case one might be justified in suspecting a lack of courage. But if a hundred, if a thousand endure the caprice of a single man, should we not rather say that they lack not the courage, but the desire to rise against him, and that such an attitude indicates indifference rather than cowardice? When not a hundred, not a thousand men, but a hundred provinces, a thousand cities, a million men, refuse to assail a single man from whom the kindest treatment received is the infliction of

serfdom and slavery, what shall we call that? Is it cowardice? Of course there is in every vice inevitably some limit beyond which one cannot go. Two, possibly ten, may fear one; but when a thousand, a million men, a thousand cities, fail to protect themselves against the domination of one man, this cannot be called cowardly, for cowardice does not sink to such a depth, any more than valour can be termed the effort of one individual to scale a fortress, to attack an army, or to conquer a kingdom. What monstrous vice, then, is this which does not even deserve to be called cowardice, a vice for which no term can be found vile enough, which nature herself disavows and our tongues refuse to name?'[53]

In underlining this question so markedly, de la Boétie shows the central problem of what he calls being 'degraded, submissive and incapable of any great deed.'[54]

De la Boétie points to several reasons that lead to this servitude and unequal relationship. First, there is the non-habit of being free. Second, is the loss of courage. And last but not least, the fact that tyrants trade on the gullibility of the populace. According to de la Boétie, people forget their need to free very easily. 'It is incredible how as soon as a people becomes subject,' affirms de la Boétie, 'it promptly falls into such complete forgetfulness of its freedom that it can hardly be roused to the point of regaining it, obeying so easily and so willingly that one is led to say, on beholding such a situation, that this people has not so much lost its liberty as won its enslavement. It is true that in the beginning men submit under constraint and by force; but those who come after them obey without regret and perform willingly what their predecessors had done because they had to. This is why men born under the yoke and then nourished and reared in slavery are content, without further effort, to live in their native circumstance, unaware of any other state or right, and considering as quite natural the condition into which they were born.'[55]

The whole of la Boétie's enterprise is based on the study of the relationship of the governed and the governing body. Thus it appears that the idea of 'servitude' and 'submission to power' is of evident importance for the background of understanding the phenomenon of 'crowd'. As Elias Canetti argues, 'A command addressed to a large number of people thus has a very special character. It is intended to make a crowd of them and, in as far as it succeeds in this, it does not arouse fear. The slogan of a demagogue, impelling people in a certain direction, has exactly the same function; it can be regarded as a command addressed to large numbers. From the point of view of the crowd, which wants to come into existence quickly and to maintain itself as a unit, such slogans are useful and indeed indispensable. The art of a speaker consists in compressing all his aims into slogans. By hammering them home, he then engenders a crowd and helps to keep it in existence. He creates the crowd and keeps it alive by a comprehensive command from above. Once he has achieved this, it scarcely matters what he demands. A speaker can insult and threaten an assemblage of people in the most terrible way and they will still love him if, by doing so, he succeeds in forming them into a crowd.'[56] As in the case of la Boétie, Canetti puts forward the question of why crowds follow the rulers. Through his study of command, Canetti refers to the concept of 'crowd' to signify a sort of general phenomenon that continues to be present in many societies. This could also refer, according to Canetti, to collective identities which bring together individuals who initially are very different from each other. According to Canetti, 'Man has a profound need to arrange and re-arrange in groups all the human beings he knows or can imagine; by dividing that loose, amorphous mass into two opposing groups he gives it a kind of density. He draws up these groups as though in battle array; he makes them exclusive and fills them with enmity for each other... At the root of the process lies the urge to form hostile packs, which, in the end, leads inevitably to actual war packs.'[57] Canetti is referring hereby at a we–they relationship, which can emerge out of the crowd logic. By bringing to the fore the antagonistic nature of political identities, turning into what Carl Schmitt calls a friend–enemy relation, any form of servility to a crowd closes down the possibility of a pluralist and agonistic democratic order automatically. It is interesting that Schmitt considers the we–they opposition as a criterion of the political, maybe because for him there is no such thing as a fully inclusive consensus. 'The challenge posed by Schmitt to the rationalist conception of the political is clearly acknowledged by Jurgen Habermas, one of the main advocates of the deliberative model, who tries to exorcize it by declaring that those who put into question the possibility of such rational consensus and who affirm that politics is a domain where one should always expect to find discord, undermine the very possibility of democracy.'[58] However, the political is so much about a rational consensus than it is about an ever-present possibility of truth-telling. This modality of ontological veridiction is found in a *parrhesiatic* mode of citizenship. In his courses at College de France, Michel Foucault refers to the Greek notion of *parrhesia* as an art of 'speaking out freely, constitutive of the figure of this other person who is indispensable for me to be able to tell the truth about myself.'[59] The political is, therefore, linked to this act of free spokenness. It is in this sense that one has to differentiate enmity from spokenness, or as Plutarch says, the 'flatterer' from the 'friend'. The friendship that *parrhesia* refers to is a civic friendship, because we always talk to the other, though not *for* the other. According to Foucault, '*parrhesia*, the act of truth, requires: first, the manifestation of a fundamental bond between the truth spoken and the thought of the person who spoke it; [second], a challenge to the bond between two interlocutors (the person who speaks the truth and the person to whom this truth is addressed). Hence this new feature of *parrhesia*: it involves some form of courage, the minimal form of which consists in the parrhesiast taking the risk of breaking and ending the relationship to the other person which was precisely what made his discourse possible.'[60]

According to the previous analysis, it appears that one of the main weaknesses of contemporary politics is the lack of courage and outspokenness. If we accept that the political cannot survive a non-agonistic relationship, then we should establish a necessary and constitutive bond between democratic citizenship and the ethics of courage. Besides the common shortcomings of electoral democracies in today's world, the main obstacle to the resurgence of the political is the lack of *parrhesiastic* citizenship and the unchallenged hegemony of fear. In the first chapter of his book *Crowds and Power*, Canetti indicates the following point about fear: 'There is nothing that man fears more than the touch of the unknown… All the distances which men create round themselves are dictated by this fear. It is only in the crowd that man can become free of this fear of being touched. That is the only situation in which fear changes into its opposite… This reversal of the fear of being touched belongs to the nature of crowds. The feeling of relief is most striking where the density of the crowd is the greatest.'[61]

Strangely, the crowd is never ruled by itself, but it is guided and governed by a few. The main idea herewith is that crowds become habituated to modes of non-thinking and non-questioning even about the most simplistic and commonplace issues. Being diverted by bread and circus, they lose their autonomy and creativity and become incapable of looking beyond appearances. This is the point Machiavelli makes in the *Discourses*: 'Men in general,' he affirms, 'are as much affected by what a thing appears to be as by what it is, indeed they are frequently influenced more by appearances than by reality.'[62] This aspect of the problem is also discussed by Hannah Arendt when she talks about the 'appearance' of the subjects in the public sphere. Appearing in public is, according to Arendt, a way for subjects to become visible to each other. But appearance is not mere reality, since there are different modes of appearance in the public space. Arendt adds, 'Only where things can be seen by many in a variety of aspects without changing their identity, so that those gathered around them know they see sameness in utter diversity, can worldly reality truly and reliably appear.'[63] This plural dimension can disappear in a lynching crowd or in totalitarian masses 'where we see all people as though they were members of one family, each multiplying and prolonging the perspective of their neighbour.'[64] Behind the mask of appearances, therefore, there are unique individuals who enact the stories of their lives.

The word 'appearance' carries at least two different but interrelated meanings in our vocabulary. First, we speak of appearance as something which is public in contrast to hidden. Second, we can identify the act of appearing in the physical spaces of the contemporary world in relation with what Guy Debord calls 'La Société du spectacle' (*The Society of the Spectacle*). Debord's first remark in the book is the following: 'The whole life of those societies in which modern conditions of production prevail presents itself as an immense accumulation of spectacles. All that once was directly lived has become mere representation.'[65] From Debord's point of view, social life has been colonized by the historical domination of commodity.

As a result, says Debord, we are witnessing the 'downgrading of being into having that left its stamp on all human endeavour. The present stage, in which social life is completely taken over by the accumulated products of the economy, entails a generalized shift from having to appearing: all effective "having" must now derive both its immediate prestige and its ultimate raison d'etre from appearances.'[66] This inverted image of the society is also present on the public scene of politics, where 'the individual, though condemned to the passive acceptance of an alien everyday reality, is thus driven into a form of madness in which, by resorting to magical devices, he entertains the illusion that he is reacting to this fate.'[67]

As such, the so-called deliberative citizens of democratic societies do not deliberate at all, but fulfill the task of what Walter Lipmann calls 'a deaf spectator in the back row [who] cannot quite manage to keep awake.'[68] If we accept Lipmann's theory, public opinion in the contemporary world is reduced to technical assumptions and affirmation about laws and regulations that influence our lives, rather than a radical and uninterrupted questioning about the nature of justice and the substance of the political in our societies. As Lipmann asserts, the citizen 'knows he is somehow affected by what is going on. Rules and regulations continually, taxes annually and wars occasionally remind him that he is being swept along by great drifts of circumstance.'[69] This statement can be the point of departure for our debate which highlights the illegitimacy of democratic governance in the absence of a true political community. If this is the case, our present effort to understand and revive the political can be analyzed as an attempt to challenge and redefine what is presented to us today as a political community. For, regardless of what the future of politics will be in the next several decades of the twenty-first century, we need to take the debate on the political beyond the narrow confines of the liberalism–libertarian–communitarian debates. As such, grasping the *kairotic* principles of the political necessitate a revolution of values which follow up the radical critique of global governance. This being so, the global conception of political community undermines the shared capacities among human beings to form a solidaristic forum of exchange by the use of speech and action. Hence, the paradox of democratic legitimacy is to consider humanity as a single *demos* by referring to the Western world as its legitimate source of political authority. And this leads to the conclusion that all particularistic claims to democratic action must be considered invalid in principle until they have been considered as legitimate by the global instances of political community. From this perspective, the problematic of the political, as an irreducible element of the political, finds itself reified by a particular definition of democracy and thereby reduced to a distinction between 'us' and 'them'. However, democracy is a political experience that does not submit to the rigid thinking of binary oppositions. Where democracy is practised, the rules of the political are defined by the absence of a communal differentiation between the same and the other. However, as we see in the contemporary world, democracy can turn into a simple game of regulations and institutions where citizens appear as an inert mass of private and de-publicized individuals who would take no pride and no interest in the development of the political.

By far, the most interesting critique of democratic formalism has been made by Carl Schmitt in his book *The Crisis of Parliamentary Democracy*. According to Schmitt, 'The situation of parliamentarism is critical today because the development of modern mass democracy has made argumentative public discussion an empty formality... The parties (which according to the text of the written constitution officially do not exist) do not face each other today discussing opinions, but as social or economic

power-groups calculating their mutual interests
and opportunities for power, and they actually
agree compromises and coalitions on this basis.
The masses are won over through a propaganda
apparatus whose maximum effect relies on an appeal
to immediate interests and passions.'[70] What Schmitt
is referring to hereby is that parties do not represent
the political, but rather seek to emphasize on their
own politics, represented by the social and economic
power. Therefore, according to Schmitt, there is an
irreducible split between the people and the parties.
Schmitt points out that 'in spite of all its coincidence
with democratic ideas and all the connections it has
to them, parliamentarianism is not democracy any
more than it is realized in the practical perspective
of expediency. If, for practical and technical reasons,
the representatives of the people can decide instead
of the people themselves, then certainly a single
trusted representative could also decide in the name
of the same people.'[71] As such, the hypocritical
nature of parliamentary liberalism as described by
Schmitt is perfectly legitimate in the understanding
of the concept of the political, though his solution
to the contradiction between democracy and the
people remains unacceptable. Schmitt's concept of
the political presupposes the distinction between
friend and enemy. As Heinrich Meier points out,
Schmitt asks the following question: 'Whom can I

at all recognize to be my enemy? Apparently only him who can place me in question. In so far as I recognize him as my enemy, I recognize that he can put me in question. And who can effectively put me in question? Only myself.'[72] Thus Schmitt not only concludes that 'I myself am my own enemy' but he also adds that: 'my brother proves to be my enemy.' He finds his example in the story of Cain and Abel, in Genesis: 'Adam and Eve had two sons, Cain and Abel. This is how the history of mankind begins. This is how the father of all things looks. That is the dialectical tension that keeps world history in motion, and world history has not yet come to an end.'[73] In other words, for Schmitt there is no meaningful self without an enemy. 'One classifies oneself by means of the enemy.' What does Schmitt teach us here? His point is that the political is constitutive of the formation of one's identity. Unlike politics, which remains alienated and blocked by its own institutions, the agonal and reciprocal nature of the political breaks through the utilitarian underpinnings of party politics. For Schmitt, party politics are similar to industrial monopolies. In his response to Richard Thoma, in the Preface to the second edition of his book, *The Crisis of Parliamentary Democracy*, he writes: 'What numerous parliaments in various European and non-European states have produced in the way of a political elite of hundreds of successive ministers justifies no great optimism. But worse and destroying almost every hope, in a few states, parliamentarianism has already produced a situation in which all public business has become an object of spoils and compromise for the parties and their followers, and politics, far from being the concern of an elite, has become the despised business of a rather dubious class of persons.' Perhaps Schmitt's arguments on the idea of the political and his critique of party politics might appear too extreme to many contemporary minds, but nevertheless, he is right to point out the monopolization of politics in so-called liberal democracies by political parties.

Leaving aside Carl Schmitt's political-theological battle, we can move beyond the thermodynamics of party politics, in order to understand, analyze and cultivate the passage from an empty space of citizenship as passive consumerism and supervised leisure to a public sphere of active participation and critical argumentation. One thing is certain: political disaster initiated and developed by political parties has brought political theory to the breaking point. Even young people who read the classical political theory of Aristotle, Machiavelli, Hobbes, Locke, Montesquieu, Kant and Hegel today, are mostly those students of philosophy and political science in European and North American universities who have the excuse of preparing for final exams and forgetting the whole canon later on. It would certainly be a vain hope to think that these thinkers find their places on the shelves of living rooms in modern condominiums. The times are simply not with the classics and their view of the political. As examples multiply in diverse national administrations and academic institutions, political *paideia* is lost and the door is opened to demagogy, infantilism and mystification. The dominant model of politics in contemporary societies is to leave the private sphere periodically for every election and to return to it after voting. Therefore, the fullest aspiration of citizenship is expressed in the simple action of voting. General suffrage is the common political stage and the self-fulfilling activity for citizens who seem to have lost the essentials of political *paideia*. This political *paideia* is always accompanied with a quest of autonomy or what Cornelius Castoriadis calls 'the explicit self-institution'. In this sense, political *paideia* is the ethos of a public domain which remains absolutely transparent and immanent. 'In other words, *paideia* is what pertains to the public presence of this society's imaginary, *stricto sensu*.'[74] Thus, in an autonomous society, *paideia* is the explicit self-questioning of the society. However, this self-questioning has been prostituted by social-historical regimes. As Castoriadis points out, 'Namely, in these regimes, the source and foundation of the law, as well as the source and foundation of each norm, value and signification, are considered transcendent in relation to the society; transcendent in an absolute way, as in monotheistic societies, and transcendent, in any case, with regard to the reality of the living society, as it happens in mythical or primitive societies (mythical not in the sense that they are societies narrated by myths, but in the sense that they are societies that base their institution on myths). And heteronomy goes hand in hand with something that is quite important for us and I will call it, for now, closure of significations; that means that the word God or the provisions that our ancestors bestowed are not debatable and they are established once and for all.'[75]

On the whole, thus, the political *paideia*, or let us call the explicit self-examination of the society, is a way to go beyond this closure of significations. It is a vital element of the political, where the people are expected to take care of their own affairs, by refusing to be represented by others and have a limited control over politics. Moreover, the crucial point in the making of the political is that it is made by prime ministers or parliamentarians, let alone in the private chambers of political parties. The political is, therefore, built on the daily function of a vibrant public sphere, which should and would eventually free all members of the political society from the constraints and limitations of traditional power and structures. It is precisely this explicit engagement of the citizens in the public space which makes the political publicness dialogical and inclusive. Let us understand it well, 'The public sphere is not just a space where private individuals appear as public, transcending their individuality and autonomy to acknowledge their commonality, reflecting and debating issues of common public concern. It is also a space where communities are forced to come together—overcoming their insularity and exclusivity and recognizing the need to connect—to reconstitute themselves as a public.'[76] Actually, the publicness of the political (unlike political power) is because of its accessibility to all. Second, because there is a permanent debate and discussion on issues of shared values and shared significance. Last but not least, the challenge of the political is to replace the multi-layered homogeneity of party politics with the heterogeneity of critical publicness. The right to critical publicness is a right of the political, not of politics. No active citizenry can function without a true consciousness of this right. Now, citizenry is not a matter of belonging, but a matter of inclusive political consciousness. It should be clear by now that the political and its explicit publicness bear close relations with the concept and practice of questioning and creating norms.

It is necessary here to make a short philosophical digression. When, in a way, we talk about the act of questioning as a political practice, we are talking about what Kant called *Methodenlehren* or paths to moral cultivation. To trace this path, Kant invites us to prepare ourselves for freedom, without taking it for granted. In the *Critique of Judgment*, Kant talks about 'producing the fitness of rational being for any purposes whatever of choosing [freedom].'[77] The critical philosophy functions here as a pedagogical activity based on the light of reason. It is accompanied with a clearing up of error and the shaping of all the undeveloped natural aptitudes of humanity. What Kant then means by the 'public use of reason', which we can consider as the highest exemplification of political *paideia*, is a form to be practiced as a very way of thinking and a critical habit of mind. In a Kantian spirit, we can add that political *paideia* is the vocation or destiny of humanity (*Bestimmung des Menschen*). In other words, the political education of humanity starts and ends with practical wisdom and critical reasoning. Without these two projects, politics would have the tendency to be violent and barbaric. The critical self-examination of humanity, therefore, is not the possession of politics, but worthiness to create and preserve the political. To follow the paths of Kant, we can also affirm education of humanity by means of political cultivation as opposed to party politics and power making.

Having established the primacy of the political over politics, the remaining task is the examination of the pedagogical means leading to the realization of the political. Here again, the pedagogical effort is directed toward cultivating maturity. This raises questions concerning the value of civic upbringing, as an individual process and as a process that a community goes through. Here, the education is not about learning facts, but how to cultivate one's judgment in order to be able to distinguish between the mediocre and the spiritually noble. In this context, the citizen is not an expert and civic education of the political, which is crucial to the life of the citizen, is not a *techne*. There is no doubt that within the concept of the political, the fellow citizen is more highly regarded than the expert politician and bureaucrat. A citizen, unlike a believer, does not believe that her truths are eternal and sent from heaven. Consequently, the practical wisdom (*phronesis*) of the political is not linked to a theoretical knowledge but to a dialogical and soul-awakening experience of individuals. As Kant says in his 1778 letter to Christian Wolke: 'The only thing necessary is not theoretical learning, but the *Bildung* of human beings, both in regard to their talents and their character.'[78] Here, education is not in the conventional sense of the term. If this is how things are in the context of the political, then education is not about repeating and imitating the already inherited values that are collectively accepted, but also being able to create new values and norms in an autonomous way. It is certainly not ideological, but it is philosophical since it is an exploration of constantly new questionings and a re-activation of the process of thinking.

The last word of this chapter is given once again to Cornelius Castoriadis whose thought calls our attention to the following: 'Philosophy shows us... that it would be silly and absurd to believe that we might ever exhaust the thinkable, the feasible or the formable, just as it shows it would be silly and absurd to set limits on the power of formation that is always present within people's psychical imagination and within the collective socio-historical imaginary. But philosophy doesn't stop us from ascertaining that humanity has already been through periods of decay and lethargy, much more insidious, to the degree they were followed, i.e., during the Roman Empire era, by what we usually call material well-being. But to the degree, frail or not, that this depends on us, and especially on those among us that think and try, as long as what we think and try to do and show to others remain true to the idea of human autonomy, then we could at least contribute to making this phase of slow lethargy as short as possible.'[79] There is an important point in what Castoriadis stresses herewith. We all have the capacity to disobey conformism and to be autonomous. However, dissenters tend to be considered in contemporary societies as anarchists, individualists, non-pragmatists and selfish loners. But in an important sense, dissenters and disobedient minds have more to contribute to the life of the political than conformist crowds who prefer not to take any risks against laws, institutions and value in what they consider as 'well-functioning systems'. As such, we should not prohibit, debar and exclude dissenters and wish them away from the public space. Most often, heretics and dissenters have been the creative spirits of history. They have been a prime source of resistance to thoughtlessness and meaninglessness in human societies.

Part II

Gandhi and Disobedience

4

GANDHI AND THE
IMPERATIVE OF DISSENT

Many decades ago, Pandit Jawaharlal Nehru, India's
first prime minister, described Mahatma Gandhi as a
person who 'seems to be the vehicle and embodiment
of some greater force of which even he is perhaps
only dimly conscious.' Nehru's affirmation was
immediately followed by an interrogation: 'Is that
the spirit of India, the accumulated spirit of the
millennia that lie behind our race, the memory of a
thousand tortured lives? ... Has he drunk somewhere
from the sacred spring of life that has given strength
to India through the ages?'[80] Undoubtedly, Gandhi's
response to Nehru's flattering words would have
been simple and modest, though there is something
true about him in this homage. As history shows us,
Gandhi, unlike many of his contemporaries, was not
a man of conformity and complacency. Quite the

contrary, both as a thinker and a practitioner, he was a disobedient mind. However, Gandhi appears to many around the world today as a spiritual man who tried to find a harmonious balance between a contemplative life and a life of action, but he tried to do this by submitting 'his views to relentless criticism, sometimes his own, but more often that of the other people.'[81]

Gandhi was a great reader of the classics, however, it is not because of his readings of Socrates and Thoreau that he is an integral representative of a disobedient mind. It was in 1907, in South Africa, that Gandhi read for the first time Henry David Thoreau's famous pamphlet, *The Duty of Civil Disobedience*. He was so impressed by Thoreau's pamphlet that he published it in paraphrase and later invited his friends and followers to read Thoreau and to become 'Thoreaus in miniature'.[82] Not surprisingly, Gandhi considered his own incarceration in South Africa as a thoreauvian adventure, since he believed that jail is the only place for a man who struggles for justice in a tyrannical state.[83] As a result, Gandhi found Thoreau's mindset very relevant to his own cause. Disobedience, as Gandhi saw it, 'was the deliberate breach of immoral statutory enactments where one invokes the sanctions of the law and invites penalties and imprisonment. This can only be practiced as a last resort and by a select few, who have the moral stature to challenge the law and to accept the consequences.'[84] Moreover, what interested Gandhi in Thoreau was his reference to the role of moral conscience in resistance against injustice. For Gandhi, the voice of conscience transcended that of the State. 'Those who obey their sense of justice while holding the reins of government are always found to be in conflict with the state.'[85] The focus of Gandhi's resistance against authority and injustice, then, was his conscience, or what he named as his 'inner voice'. For Gandhi, the inner voice was the voice of truth which could be heard only by experimenting and trained individuals. Hence, says Gandhi, 'according to my definition, a murderer cannot cite inner voice in defense of his act.'[86] Here again, we see the role of ethics in Gandhian politics. This is how we can evaluate the broader contribution of Gandhi to disobedient and protest movements around the world. That is why, for seven decades, Gandhi has been an inspiration to several generations of nonviolent freedom fighters in the West and in the East. His philosophy of nonviolence and his quest for peace and harmony among individuals and nations is shared by civic actors and public intellectuals around the world. From Martin Luther King Jr. and His Holiness the Dalai Lama to the young activists of the Tahrir

Square, and for all those fighting against all forms of injustice, Gandhi has been the most celebrated and cited political thinker of the twentieth century. The language of Gandhism has been more popularized but, at the same time, it is more confused than the mind of Gandhi as a thinker. Maybe that is why, all through his life, Gandhi strongly rejected the concept of Gandhism. In a speech at Seva Sangh in March 3, 1936 he declared: 'I have conceived no such thing as Gandhism. I am not an exponent of any sect. I never claimed to have originated any philosophy. Nor am I endeavouring to do so.'[87]

If Gandhi is beyond Gandhism, it is simply because, neither as a thinker nor as a politician, is he interested in constructing a mass ideology. Politics for Gandhi means the art of organizing the society and a form of resistance against evil. As a form of resistance, Gandhi developed the political into a weapon of mass protest and civil disobedience. Though influenced directly by Thoreau, the Gandhian view of civil disobedience was different from the former in several respects. According to Anthony Parel, 'First, it was grounded in truth (satya) and was part of a broader programme of the reform of civil society... Secondly, it was different in its attitude towards violence. It adhered to nonviolence in principle, a principle that was flexibly applied... Thirdly, it required a minimum degree of moral fitness, involving the practice of certain virtues... Fourthly, it accepted the punishment consequent upon disobedience without complaint... Finally, Gandhian civil disobedience had to be complemented by the reform of civil society.'[88] This is where Gandhi's concept of disobedience grounded in truth appears as a relevant idea for today's world. For Gandhi, life, as the title of his autobiography suggests, is an 'experiment with truth'. However, Gandhi did not consider truth as a pre-established concept. That is why in Gandhian theory of ethics, the inner voice is an encounter with truth. It was this voice within that led Gandhi to the conclusion that life is a quest for truth and a struggle for justice. As such, Gandhi transformed truth from an abstract philosophical concept into an ethical principle of action. Perhaps one of Gandhi's greatest accomplishments was to replace fear of authority with courage to resist and overcome it. According to Gandhi, 'real swaraj will come not by the acquisition of authority by a few, but by the acquisition of the capacity by all to resist authority when abused...by educating the masses to a sense of their capacity to regulate and control authority.'[89]

What is so striking about Gandhi's criticism of the concept of authority is how he applies the idea of education as a form of capacity building. Moreover, since his campaigns for satyagraha in

South Africa, Gandhi spoke of his sense of ethical responsibility as a way to stand firm against an unjust law. Actually, in Gandhi's view, what revealed the ethical strength and the transformative power of satyagraha to the Indians and to the British was the idea of self-respect as the outcome of fearless disobedience. As Gandhi put it, 'The power of suggestion is such, that a man at last becomes what he believes himself to be... Believing ourselves to be strong, two clear consequences result from it. Fostering the idea of strength, we grow stronger and stronger everyday. With the increase in our strength, our Satyagraha too becomes more effective.'[90] In a decisive speech given on September 11, 1906 in South Africa, Gandhi acknowledged the principle factors of his experiment in disobedience. Though history has retained the concept of satyagraha as the outcome of what Gandhi considered as the ethical strength to resist dehumanization, the real tool that Gandhi developed from this experience was the subversive ethical vice of disobedience. As far as Gandhi was concerned, learning to disobey British rule as much as false values of modern civilization, like wealth and utility, would help Indians to come to ethical maturity. 'So swaraj could neither be imposed on nor given to India; rather, all Indians had to experience those values for themselves and learn to rule themselves—and only on such a new ethical foundation of transformed individuals would an India worth having arise.'[91] In summary, for Gandhi, autonomy and maturity go hand in hand. Therefore, where there is maturity as self-respect of the individual, we can also find immediately the idea of freedom of critical reasoning and the freedom of self-transforming.

In effect, however, what Gandhi understands by swaraj is the capacity for self-questioning and self-creation as socio-historical practices of freedom. As such, the freedom to reject the unjust law and to refigure the political is, for Gandhi, a way to respond creatively to the sovereignty of the State. Gandhi did not think much of the modern State. 'It was highly centralized and intolerant of self-governing communities. Enjoying the monopoly of violence, it relied on the use or threat of force and did not activate the moral energies of its citizens. It was impersonal and bureaucratic, a "soulless machine" which ruled by means of rigid rules and discouraged personal responsibility and initiative. It made a fetish of territorial integrity, thought little of sacrificing human lives in defending every inch of it and jealously demanded its citizens' exclusive loyalty.'[92] For Gandhi, the problem with the modern State is its monolithic nature which creates a good deal of violence. He, therefore, envisaged a State based on nonviolence. 'The predominantly nonviolent state is characterized by Gandhi as decentralized, democratic, self-regulated, controlling its institutes of political power, independent politically, economically and spiritually.'[93] Gandhi was extremely anxious about the role of the State and the increase of its power based on fear. But while he considered that the State had limited the freedom of individuals, he rejected at the same time unrestricted individualism as the law of the jungle.

Interestingly, Gandhi is one of the rare thinkers of modernity who does not follow the idea of consent as a common justification of political obligation. This is where Gandhi separates from the liberal tradition of thought. It is hard to underline the force of the concept of consent on the Gandhian mind, especially because Gandhi does not identify democracy with the imposition of a lawful obligation upon a political community. That is why, in the Gandhian theory of democracy, there is simply no reference to an element of public authority based on the logic of consent. For Gandhi, therefore, the moral duty of citizens, as a condition of good governance, is not seen in the act of continuous legitimation of the State. In a deeper sense, according to Gandhi, the democratic citizen owes its final allegiance to its own capacity of self-government. This, of course, gives the disobedient mind the benefit of a substantial doubt and criticism of the State and to hold all forms of obligation in regard to the authority of the State invalid. Thus, the Gandhian legitimation of disobedience through the widening of boundaries of citizenship are only ways to remind the citizens that the political process which decides whether an act of disobedience is right or wrong is not infallible. However, Gandhi's theory of disobedience does not turn him into an anarchist. But as Bhikhu Parekh points out clearly, 'like many a moral idealist, Gandhi found it difficult to appreciate the role of coercion in social life and to come to terms with the state.'[94] Gandhi was realistic enough to recognize that to liberate India from 'the dreaded prospect of anarchy', the best way was to revitalize the political space through the active participation of each individual.[95] From Gandhi's point of view, to be a citizen one needs to engage in public life. Besides, the impetus for participation and transformation is not supposed to come downward from the State to the society. Therefore, the good of the society is in the hands of its members, not that of the State. That is to say, the motor of change in the Gandhian political theory is the individual, not the State. But the individual can only be an agent of change for the better when it operates in conjunction with every other member of civil society. This interconnectedness among members of civil society requires not only adherence to nonviolence but also a minimum degree of self-discipline and moral obligation. In other words, the Gandhian attitude towards the political is founded on the basic idea that both legality and the act of disobeying it need to be grounded in truth (satya) and involve practice of virtue. Evidently, Gandhi's novel philosophical argument is that the secret to the self-transformation of the political is truth. Paraphrasing John Ruskin (another author which he discovered and read while he was in South Africa), Gandhi reminds his readers that 'India was once looked upon as a golden land, because Indians then were people of sterling worth. The land is the same but the people have changed and that is why it has become arid. To transform it into a golden land again we must transmute ourselves into gold by leading a life of virtue... If, therefore, every Indian makes it a point to follow truth always, India will achieve *swarajya* as a matter of course.'[96]

What Gandhi considers as the realization of truth in the realm of the political is to have a spiritual intervention in the world. In this sense, disobedience informed by true spirituality is in the service of justice and nonviolence. The practice of disobedience, in the sense of overcoming the most evil of all evils—greed for power—should be mindful of the need to cultivate a spirituality that promotes nonviolence. In a second sense, disobedience for Gandhi means the spiritual exercise of the political in terms of rights and duties. Truly speaking, from the Gandhian perspective, there is no self-rule without the duty to disobey. In general, for Gandhi, the art of disobedience is to improve the quality of justice in a society, by upgrading the moral temper of social and political institutions. As such, Gandhi is perfectly conscious of the fact that the habit of obedience to the State contributes to the rise of conformism and passivity of the individual citizen. This signifies a fundamental change in Gandhi's vision of social obligation and political awareness. For Gandhi, political obligation is not the only sort of consideration relevant to a determination of how we ought to act within a political community. Actually, for him, it seems inconceivable that a citizen should recognize an ethical foundation for her action, while failing to recognize the act of disobeying as a social duty that binds each member of the political community to support justice. However, rights and duties do not exhaust the subject matter of disobedience. There is nothing paradoxical about such a conclusion when one frees oneself from the view of obligation as a narrow and rigid set of requirements and prohibitions. That is to say, for Gandhi, obligation and obedience remain in need of justification more than disobedience, which frees a person from the political trap of remaining a citizen. In other words, we are not necessarily on a morally safe ground by obeying the law and the State. It is in this spirit that the motto of Ralph Waldo Emerson makes sense when he writes: 'good men must not obey the law too well.'[97]

Gandhi understood well that disobedience is a long-term perspective that cannot be fulfilled immediately. 'A man is obliged to follow the legislation. But Gandhi is convinced that there should be no place for blind obedience to any law, because they can be unjust and violate the idea and the principles of highest law. We admit that unjust laws exist. It happens these days that many things which are legal are not just.'[98] Gandhi persisted that we should follow legislation only when it doesn't contradict our conscience. He agreed with Thoreau that the sound of conscience must always be higher than any law; unjust laws should be disobeyed. Gandhi considers it a duty to disobey unjust laws. 'I have found that it is our first duty to render voluntary obedience to law, but whilst doing that duty, I have also seen that when law fosters untruth it becomes a duty to disobey it.'[99]

If Gandhi develops the idea of disobedience as an ethical imperative, he also considers education as the only way to promote the Socratic virtue of questioning. For Gandhi, education is a dissenting agent of change and transformation. It is the key player in character-building and nation-building. According to Gandhi, an education that does not promote quality of life and excellence is worthless. Gandhi underlines: 'The ancient aphorism, "education is that which liberates," is true today as it was before. Education here does not mean mere spiritual knowledge, nor does liberation signify only spiritual liberation after death. Knowledge includes all training that is useful for the services of mankind and liberation means freedom from all manner of servitude, even in the present life. Servitude is of two kinds: slavery to domination from outside and to one's own artificial needs. The knowledge acquired in the pursuit of this ideal alone constitutes true study.'[100] In other words, Gandhi considers education as a means to creating harmony and exchange with others. But he is also very conscious of the fact that education develops the questioning capacities of a disobedient mind which can resist injustice, untruth and violence. Therefore, only through education can a disobedient personality be developed, which can bring ethics into politics and make individuals sensitive to the issue of the value-crisis in our world. We see here the true task of education in Gandhian thought as a creative act of resistance against relativism, which covers all the departments of life. Gandhi is aware of the fact that education is not about memorizing books or accumulating knowledge, but about learning to think. This is what he writes in an article entitled 'What is Education?' in *Navajivan* on February 28, 1926: 'The English word "education" etymologically means "drawing out". That means an endeavour to develop our latent talents. The same is the meaning of kelavani, the Gujarati word for education. When we say that we develop a certain thing, it does not mean that we change its kind or quality, but that we bring out the qualities latent in it. Hence "education" can also mean "unfoldment".'[101]

Gandhi also understands education as enlightenment. He affirms that 'education without enlightenment is like a wall without a foundation or, to employ an English saying, like a whited sepulchre.'[102] By 'enlightenment', Gandhi understands the moral progress of mankind. As such, his experiments with education transform constantly into self-transforming experiments of community life. The purpose of education, according to Gandhi, is two things: First, daring to think and to question reality. Second, learning the art of living peacefully and in coexistence with others. But the question remains: What are we to make of education in the making of a disobedient mind? Not surprisingly, for Gandhi, education is a way of innovating the inherited ideas of our ancestors. Actually, this is what Gandhi did over half a century throughout his political career. 'I believe,' he says, 'it is our duty to augment the legacy of our ancestors and to change it into current coin and make it acceptable to the present age.'[103] However, in his act of innovation, Gandhi put more weight on the process of revolutionizing the ancestral values, rather than just following them blindly. As evidence of Gandhi's idea of the 'revolution of values', Sunil Khilnani points out Gandhi's rejection of the idea 'that past history was a source for defining future possibilities or orienting present action.' As a matter of fact, 'and in contrast to nationalists who sought to construct a reliable future out of a selected past, Gandhi expressed profound distrust for the historical genre... Gandhi refused the ubiquitous ground of all nationalisms, the discourse of history, and created a distinctive definition of Indian identity...his appeal to pre-existing local beliefs and identities in order to create a larger, Indian one was tied to an idea of *swadeshi*, a patriotism based on a respect for the everyday material world inhabited by most on the subcontinent... This ambition for a self-producing community was strongly moralizing, and dispensed entirely with the idea of a territorial nation state.'[104]

Gandhi's idea of swadeshi, like that of his system of education, was not based on one's own interest, but rather on that of an empathic approach to the other. 'For him, the principle underlying this virtue was that of neighbourliness. "A man's first duty," he argued, was "to his neighbour". This did not mean hatred of the foreigner or partiality toward one's own. It meant that in serving one's neighbour one served the whole world.'[105] The question of how to serve the interests of others while remaining faithful to one's conscience is at the heart of Gandhi's ethical philosophy. As a result, those who truly understand Gandhi's idea of empathy would necessarily find it realizable in action. The critical point here is Gandhi's belief in the connection between means and ends in all the actions taken by us. This brings us to say that, like nonviolence, disobedience is at the same time a means and an end. It concerns the question of questioning and whether it has a subservient role in the making of a political community. Gandhi did not think that the claim that "the end justifies the means" would hold in the long run. For him, then, using questioning as a means to put an end to questioning itself would be self-defeating. This, far from being an act of questioning, would be an act of violation of all questions and doubts. It is actually at this point that Gandhi's theory of nonviolence gains traction. By nonviolence, Gandhi meant not just love of the enemy, but mainly the questioning of his values.

Gandhi offers us herewith an innovative idea of disobedience, not only as a critique of authority, but also as a revolution of values. In this case, the purpose of disobedience would be to disrupt the normality of values by promoting self-awareness in the social network of human exchange. In other words, disobedience, as a spirit and as an act, has an ethical significance more than just a tactical value in nonviolent struggle. Disobedience is a just action when it squares with the moral law. To paraphrase Martin Luther King Jr., any disobedience that uplifts human personality is just, any disobedience that degrades human personality is unjust. Disobedience is just, in the Gandhian sense of the term, because it is the governance of the individual by the individual. As a result, from a Gandhian point of view, we need a disobedient state of mind to end up with *political swaraj*. Swaraj, as self-rule, helps to create a self-enlightened citizenry which remains disobedient and resistant in regard to the abusive laws of men and gods. This, in a nutshell, is the substance of Gandhi's philosophy of disobedience.

Now the question remains: Is Gandhi a disobedient Indian? The answer would be positive. Gandhi is a disobedient mind in his intellectual attitude towards the modern time and as long as he applies what he calls the 'acid test of reason' to all socio-political and religious ideas and opinions, including his own. But if we ask the second question: Is Gandhi an anarchist? The answer would be negative, since Gandhi's critique of the modern State and bureaucratic authority makes sense only in the framework of what he calls 'an enlightenment democracy'. The power of an enlightened democracy is correlative with the civic disobedient virtue that demands the laws and institutions of democracy to be revisited and revised. In this sense, Gandhian democracy is a political community which exists in a dialogical process. Therefore, a Gandhian disobedient mind is not only a questioning spirit, but it is also a creative and dynamic force that keeps the crucial question of questioning open.

5

THE DISOBEDIENT INDIAN

The question of questioning is no longer a part of our everyday social and political grammar in recent times. One of the most serious and frequent opinions against the act of questioning is the absurd belief that if everyone questions everything, the result would be chaos and the destruction of human civilization. However, if there is only one point which is true in this assertion, it is the reference to the fact that human civilization is walking dangerously on a tightrope. But there has certainly not been any excess in exercising the art of questioning. In today's world, a dissenter who questions the establishment is a lonely hero. This is a point of anguish when it is no longer questionable to rely on false convictions rather than on true questions. Whether that anguish is fundamentally ridiculous or respectful will depend upon one's vision. But this should remind us of what Gandhi says about the five stages in every movement: first comes indifference; second, ridicule; third, abuse; fourth, repression and fifth, respect. And he adds, if a movement does not survive the fourth stage, it has no real chance of securing respect. This is why we can continue to believe that the spirit of questioning will take time and no civilization can live without practising the art of questioning.

Another question which is raised at this level of the discussion concerns the dignity of suffering in a just questioning. It goes without saying that, like civil disobedience, philosophical questioning too must not be undertaken without a scrupulous moral concern—simply because the common factors in civil disobedience and philosophical questioning are reliance upon moral conscience and civic virtue. Gandhi knew that both are needed. The appeal to one's conscience is necessary in the Socratic act of questioning, but it is limited when it comes to the creative institution of a political community. An individual cannot have a conscience as a whole, no more than society as a whole can have a conscience, without self-examination and self-transformation that are morally enhanced. As such, the Gandhian philosophy of resistance at its best represents a vindication of the empathic capacities of human beings in the face of evil. Gandhi's theory of resistance and disobedience is distinctive in that he sought to incorporate in it the right to be disloyal. In an article entitled 'The Duty of Disloyalty' he writes, 'There is no halfway house between active loyalty and active disloyalty... In these days of democracy there is no such thing as active loyalty to a person. You are, therefore, loyal or disloyal to institutions. When, therefore, you are disloyal you seek not to destroy persons but institutions.'[106] Here, the resistance is made possible by an ethical voice and an implicit questioning of the social and political institutions. From a Gandhian perspective, critique of the political represents a challenge to the idea of authority. Therefore, the underlying principles of Gandhian nonviolent resistance are the very notions of moral agency, in terms of insistence on truth and learning to listen to the voice of one's conscience, and nonviolent political intervention in the public realm, in the direction of self-government. Gandhi further thought that the means of achieving the political as the art of organizing the society—in contradistinction from politics as the greed of power (which encircles us like the coil of a snake)—needed to be examined and practised in a different consideration. From Gandhi's point of view, there would always be a need for spiritual intervention in the domain of the political. Far from being a religious attitude or a divine intervention in the sovereignty of human beings, the Gandhian principle of 'spiritualization of the political' can be regarded as a form of interconnecting the political to the ethical. This is where Gandhi's experiments with the political are defined by him as his 'experiments with truth'. He discovered as the result of his experiments with the political that 'the good will, combined with self-sacrifice, was intended to "open the ears" of opponents and lead them to a truthful dialogue.'[107] Gandhi's insistence on an empathic dialogue with the Other was, for him, a call on multiple perspectives on truth or what the Jains called *Anekantavada*. This is well exemplified by his ban on violent resistance. In other words, speaking of his 'experiments with truth' Gandhi points us to the political essence of this truth which is both multiple and shared. For Gandhi, truth as a shared political value is examined and adopted through the exercise of dialogue. Here, Gandhi's model is Socratic *par excellence*. 'Gandhi saw Socrates as sharing his own cause of telling the *truth* and he called his paraphrase "Story of a satyagrahi" (translated as "soldier of truth"). Socrates told the truth to his compatriots about their own defects... Gandhi presented Plato's Socrates in 1908 as a practitioner of *satyagraha*, by 1909 in *Hind Swaraj* he had analyzed his own practice further, and recognized soul-force as imposing the constraints of hurting no one else.'[108] It goes without saying that the critical question for Gandhi is to try to bring about the mandatory coordination of the Socratic questioning on truth and the ethical means of the political. It is only through such a coordination that the civic virtues of the citizens gain the power and the legitimacy to put into question the legitimacy and authority of the State. Therefore, Gandhi's philosophy of resistance in its depth is concerned more with the practice of the civic virtues of the citizens rather than the *raison d'état*. Thus, what we see in Gandhi's theoretical and practical approach to the question of the political is an epistemological inversion of the key principles of modern political thought which dismisses civic friendship in the name of the guarantee of individual liberties in the private sphere. As Anthony Parel discusses, 'Gandhi's political philosophy is not only a means of understanding the fundamental truths about political phenomena, but also a means of realizing, or at least attempting to realize, these truths in action. The realization of political truths should occur not only in the lives of individual citizens but also in the operations of the political and economic institutions... Those who truly understand Gandhi's political philosophy feel an obligation to put it into practice.'[109]

Turning to Gandhi's own words, the teleological

framework of his entire philosophy of resistance is based on his understanding of what he underlines as 'democratic swaraj'. 'It must be remembered,' affirms Gandhi, 'that it is not Indian Home Rule depicted in the book [*Hind Swaraj*] that I am placing before India. I am placing before the nation parliamentary, i.e. democratic *swaraj*.'[110] Elsewhere he describes swaraj as 'a capacity to declare independence at will...totally consistent with national self-respect and it provides for the highest growth of the nation.'[111] As basic as it is in Gandhi's philosophy of resistance, swaraj is not a neutral concept. It is a mode of 'political self-hood'. Therefore, swaraj is more a duty to resist, rather than a right to be free. According to Gandhi, to resist is to be autonomous. An individual is autonomous when she dares to think differently. Therefore, swaraj, in the Gandhian sense of the term, is an enlightened self-rule. Gandhi calls it a 'disciplined rule from within.'[112] We can find herewith the reference to the Socratic questioning of the political, followed by the Gandhian conception of civic virtue. However, the secret of the Gandhian self-rule lies in 'one's rule over one's own mind'.[113] Then and only then, self-rule or autonomy brings self-awareness and consciousness of one's political obligations towards the others. Because of this, thus, individual self-transformation is tied to the self-transformative nature of the political. 'If we become free, India is free. And in this thought you have a definition of swaraj. It is swaraj when we learn to rule ourselves.'[114] From the Gandhian perspective, no society can be autonomous without autonomous individuals who know how to rule themselves. But how can individuals rule themselves without eradicating inequality, injustice and ignorance? Thus, the act of disobeying unjust laws is not only in order to respect the concept of law in general, but also to educate the citizens on issues such as liberty and responsibility. Interestingly, for Gandhi, swaraj is more than mere freedom from restraint. 'His swaraj allowed no such irresponsible freedom, but demanded rather a rigorous moulding of the self and a heavy sense of responsibility.'[115] In the Gandhian sense of resistance, this sense of responsibility is always accompanied by an acute idea of questioning the unjust law and disobeying the evil authority, while enlarging the space of freedom for others. As such, from a Gandhian point of view, when we consider the idea of obeying or disobeying a law, we need to raise the question of the moral and political limitations of its authority. Accordingly, all forms of resistance against authority are also modes of seeking truth and harmonious exchange. That is why, a nonviolent resistant or a disobedient rebel who fights against oppression cannot be truthful by committing violence. Albert Camus understood this perfectly when he wrote, 'If rebellion exists, it is because falsehood, injustice, and violence are part of the rebel's condition. He cannot, therefore, absolutely claim not to kill or lie, without renouncing his rebellion and accepting, once for all, evil and murder. But no more can he agree to kill and lie, since the inverse reasoning which would justify murder and violence would also destroy the reasons for his insurrection.'[116]

No disobedience is practised in the name of wrongs. The rebels always fight for the cause of justice and of rights. However, failing to believe in a minimum of shared moral values leaves the disobedient mind with the danger of violence. Therefore, the Gandhian philosophy of resistance encourages those who are struggling for democratic swaraj to increase peace and nonviolence in the public realm. Nevertheless, we should not forget that an act of rebellion and disobedience is justified by the persistent presence of authoritative mediocrity and conformism in our world. In a world where politics has become a form of non-thinking and non-acting, disobeying is an act of excellence. On the other hand, it should be well understood, that not all forms of disobedience are paths to moral resistance. Frankly speaking, whatever else it does or it doesn't do, a re-empowered concept of disobedience by the Gandhian philosophy of resistance seems to offer a solution to the two major political problems of today's world: meaninglessness and thoughtlessness. Following Gandhi, we can look into the realm of the political as the quintessential mode of harmonious exchange at moments of crisis, when politics needs to become re-political, that is when we need to re-establish the contract between thought and freedom. But the question to ask would be: is Gandhi's philosophy of resistance enough to ensure the consolidation of the political and the existential security of the disobedient mind? Probably not fully, 'although it contains a superior ethic that classical liberalism no longer offers and radical democracy has not yet developed.'[117]

Today's politics must recognize that there may be a third choice, the Gandhian one, rather than conformist and complacent obedience on the one hand and political violence on the other. Though the task of incorporating Gandhi into contemporary political thought and comparative political theory seems considerable, the project is not impossible.

Last but not least, resistance is a mode of questioning, not an act of excessive passion. Gandhi was very well aware of this after the tragedy of Chauri-Chaura. He declared, 'If we are not to evolve violence out of nonviolence, it is quite clear that we must hastily retrace our steps and re-establish an atmosphere of peace.'[118] And a few weeks before his assassination he underlined, 'I must not flatter myself with the belief—nor allow friends like you to entertain the belief—that I have exhibited any heroic and demonstrable nonviolence in myself. All I can claim is that I am sailing in that direction without a moment's stop. This confession should strengthen your belief in nonviolence and spur you and friends like you to action along the path.'[119]

Gandhi understood that history is more than the sum of actions of those who make it. That is why he believed in nonviolence as a spiritual effort rather than a heroic enterprise. When Louis Fischer asked him about the influence of his doctrine he responded: 'I think my influence is due to the fact I pursue the truth. That is my goal... Truth is not merely a matter of words. It is really a matter of living the truth.'[120] For Gandhi, the genuine politics worthy of the name is simply a matter of serving truth and serving the community. This is a public space in which nonviolence is an imperative rather than a mere policy. What is remarkable about Gandhi's approach to the essence of the political, rather than a strategic move towards politics as power making, is not only its originality, but also its overall harmonious vision directed towards a true revolution of values. Many years later, Martin Luther King Jr. would come back to Gandhi, believing that a revolution of values would prove an effective strategy for blacks in America, and say: 'The stability of the large world house which is ours will involve a revolution of values to accompany the scientific and freedom revolutions engulfing the earth. We must rapidly begin the shift from a "thing"-oriented society to a "person"-oriented society. When machines and computers, profit motives and property rights, are considered more important than people, the giant triplets of racism, materialism and militarism are incapable of being conquered. A civilization can flounder as readily in the face of moral and spiritual bankruptcy as it can through financial bankruptcy.'[121] In an ironic way, the Gandhian revolution of values saw its true expression in the disobedient mind and action of Martin Luther King Jr. Ultimately, both Gandhi and King left us with a testament which remains the basic issue of our human journey of freedom.

CONCLUSION

TOWARDS A GANDHIAN
PHILOSOPHY OF DISSENT

The Gandhian philosophy of dissent and disobedience is a Socratic moment of politics. In this sense, Gandhi shares with the ancient Athenians the idea that politics is a shared experience and a space to examine truth. In other words, Gandhi's real philosophical and political challenge is to make both politics and ethics truthful by creating a bridge between the two. As such, Gandhi described his conception of true citizenship as 'the reign of self-imposed law of moral restraint.' In fact, it was not a sectarian ethics that, according to Gandhi, was to be fused with politics, but what Gandhi called 'the highest moral law'. He referred to the two sides of his ethics as truth and nonviolence. Moreover, he described an ethical action as 'a matter of duty' and rejected any action which was promoted by a theological mindset. Not surprisingly, Gandhi frequently expressed his deep conviction that politics and ethics were inextricably interlinked and that their separation resembled the separation of body and soul. Gandhi was, in this respect, one of the few political leaders of his generation to also be a moral leader. Maybe that is why Gandhi's attachment to any kind of ideology and theology is limited. Politics for him is identified with ethics rather than any kind of ideology. Therefore, Gandhi's major concept of the 'political' is not an absolutist concept. In essence, Gandhi's conception of the political is not a narrow dogma, but an ethical enterprise. It is, thus, the ethical which is the basis of all action, and truth is the substance of all morality. As a result, for Gandhi, the end of the political is to ethicalize the public realm. As such, Gandhian politics is fundamentally an ethical politics, a spiritual experimentation with truth which is situated beyond politics and mediated through self-transformation. Perhaps the Gandhian goal of spiritualizing politics finds its major exemplifications in the principles and values of responsibility, civility, and toleration. 'The golden rule of conduct,' writes Gandhi, 'is mutual toleration, seeing that we will never all think alike and we shall see Truth in fragment and from different angles of vision. Conscience is not the same thing for all. Whilst, therefore, it is a good guide for individual conduct, imposition of that conduct upon all will be an insufferable interference with everybody's freedom of conscience.'[122]

Gandhi's philosophy of resistance and dissent invites us to 'live in truth' while practising the political in contradistinction to politics. This is a reminder of what Vaclav Havel underlined as 'living in truth' in a post-totalitarian state of mind. As Havel puts it succinctly here, the overwhelming problem is to confront the political power by inviting people to live in truth and justice, and for decency. According to Havel: 'Individuals...need not accept the lie. It is enough for them to have accepted their life with it and in it. For by this very fact, individuals confirm the system, fulfill the system, make the system, are the system.'[123] Havel shows brilliantly how the system successfully captures the lived experience of individuals in a post-totalitarian State by giving them the illusion of being part of a silent contract. 'But the real sphere of potential politics in the post-totalitarian system is elsewhere: in the continuing and cruel tension between the complex demands of that system and the aims of life, that is, the elementary need of human beings to live, to a certain extent at least, in harmony with themselves, that is, to live in a bearable way, not to be humiliated by their superiors and officials, not to be continually watched by the police, to be able to express themselves freely, to find an outlet for their creativity, to enjoy legal security, and so on.'[124] For Havel, what appears as an embryonic act of dissent is not to become a player in the game of a post-totalitarian State, while defending one's dignity and regaining one's sense of responsibility. This is clearly a moral act which is defined by Havel as 'living within truth'. Havel analyzes the essence of 'living within the truth' while examining the various dimensions of what he calls 'the power of the powerless'. He writes: 'When I speak of living within truth, I naturally do not have in mind only products of conceptual thought, such as a protest or a letter written by a group of intellectuals. It can be any means by which a person or a group revolts against manipulation: anything from a letter by intellectuals to a workers' strike, from a rock concert to a student demonstration, from refusing to vote in the farcical elections, to making an open speech at some official congress, or even a hunger strike, for instance. If the suppression of the aims of life is a complex process, and if it is based on the multifaceted manipulation of all expressions of life then, by the same token, every free expression of life indirectly threatens the post-totalitarian system politically, including forms of expression to which, in other social systems, no one would attribute any potential political significance, not to mention explosive power.'[125]

Gandhi's theory of satyagraha implies, first and foremost, an abiding commitment to the soul force of a person who chooses an ethical course of action in the most immoral environment. As he mentions, 'The only condition of a successful use of this force is a recognition of the existence of the soul as apart from the body and its permanent nature. And this recognition must amount to a living faith and not mere intellectual grasp.'[126] After all, from Gandhi's point of view, satyagrahic action is an appeal to one's own conscience, where the ethical principles are overpowered in contradistinction to the meaning of an incomplete conventional political power. In Gandhi's mind, democratizing politics meant not only the struggle for Indian home-rule but mainly taking nonviolent action on coercive power relations and unjust social structures. Simply because for him, the stability of human civilization, the democratic potential of a community and the moral dignity of individuals depend on challenging the evils of the growing gap between ethics and politics. In this endeavour lies, for Gandhi, the revolution of values which comes from responsible thinking, attentiveness to one's inner voice and a deep sense of empathy.

Today, the key problem in the political organization of our world is that we want to build or consolidate democracy only on rule of law. But

democracy is much more than 'thin paper'. According
to Martin Luther King Jr., '[D]emocracy transformed
from thin paper to thick action is the greatest form
of government on earth.'[127] Democracy is born
out of a sentiment of responsibility and solidarity
with the suffering humanity. This reminds us of
the inherent fragility of human existence and the
frailty of the human political condition. That is
why Gandhi is very conscious about the fact that
the cultivation of an 'enlarged pluralism' requires
the creation of institutions and practices, where the
voice and perspective of everyone can be articulated,
tested and transformed. As such, Gandhi still has the
disturbing capacity to unsettle our fixed categories,
to shake our inherited conceptual habits, and to
let us see world in a new light. The key to this
is, of course, the connection between the political
and disobedience. Again, within the framework of
shared sovereignty, Gandhi believes that the centre
of gravity of modern politics needs to be shifted
back from the idea of material power and wealth
to righteousness and truthfulness. In his criticism of
modernity, Gandhi analyzes modern civilization as
promoting the ideals of power and wealth that are
based on individual self-centeredness, and causing
the loss of community bonds that are contrary to
the moral and spiritual common good (dharma).
In his mind, there is an equal moral responsibility

to obey shared sovereignty as there is to disobey absolute sovereignty based on unjust laws. The difference between the two has to do with the moral nature and the democratic formulation of the obeyed law. Democracy, to be worthy of obedience, must be democratically structured so that every citizen could re-examine it. What is more, if society is to move upward towards autonomy, it has to undergo the Gandhian acid test of reason. What Gandhi calls 'the acid test of reason' is actually a critical approach to cultural and religious values in our societies in order to see how they are able to consider, empathically, the otherness of the other. It is from this acid test of reason, i.e. a critical examination, that Gandhi derived the idea of satyagraha, the practice of nonviolent resistance. And, so, with this thought, I return to my initial idea that the core idea of Gandhi's philosophy of resistance is his unshakeable conviction that it is no longer possible to organize the political without disobedience. Gandhi is pre-eminently a thinker and practitioner of disobedience, who could no more be understood outside the framework of the political than Donald Trump, Recep Tayyip Erdogan and Nicolás Maduro Moros might be understood as anything other than figures heavily invested in the life of power politics.

Today, Mahatma Gandhi remains a relevant

thinker of disobedience, not only because of his theory and practice of nonviolence, but also because of the way he defended all his life the Socratic art of questioning the political. Nothing about his approach is doctrinaire or a priori. Everything he claims about the importance of individual autonomy and political freedom, for human life, for modern living, is tested by experience and by his disobedient mind. Everybody knows that Gandhi's ideas evolved through experience from a highly simplistic view to more mature, sophisticated and relevant propositions. Gandhi equates experimentation with the attainment of maturity through the use of reason. For him, maturity consists in individuals taking over responsibility for using their critical rationality. For Gandhi, one can say, critical rationality consists in the unflinching examination of our most cherished beliefs and confronting assumptions. Therefore, Gandhi's heroic break with conformism and complacency opens up the possibility for a disobedient mindset, which would provide a minimum of critical structure for human action. In one sense, Gandhi's political thought can be conceived of as more comprehensive, critical and constructive than any ordinary theory of politics because, according to Gandhi, it saw more acutely and profoundly into the nature of common community. Gandhi, though a spiritual practitioner, was not tied by the laws, regulations and revelations of his own or any particular social and religious community. He believed that self-centredness in religious matters, as in political matters, created prejudice and misunderstanding. This is the language he used in an article in *Indian Opinion* in 1907: 'If the people of different religions grasp the real significance of their own religion they will never hate the people of any religion other than their own...there may be many religions, but the true aim of all is the same.'[128] For Gandhi, God was not a monopoly of any religion. As such, there is no trace of proselytizing or dogmatism in Gandhi's proclamation of his spirituality.

Therefore, Gandhi's concept of religion was not bound by any dogmatic behaviour and was not confined to temples, churches, books, rituals and other outer forms. As such, Gandhi's critique of an ideologized religion led him to a concept of the spiritual which found its expression in the 'spiritualization of politics'. For Gandhi, the aim of spiritualizing politics was constructing the future of 'human living together'. He, therefore, understood religion as a morally conscientious and socially responsible exercise of spirituality. He believed that every social and political opportunity must be made use of to forge a harmony among communities. As mentioned previously, for Gandhi, a culture or a religious tradition that denied individual freedom in the name of unity or purity was coercive and unacceptable. When women were stoned to death in Afghanistan for allegedly committing adultery, Gandhi criticized it, saying that 'this particular form of penalty cannot be defended on the ground of its mere mention in the Koran.'[129] and he added, "every formula of every religion has in this age of reason to submit to the acid test of reason and universal justice if it is to ask for universal assent."[130]

More generally, Gandhi's political thought is not bound to any particular religious or secular polity. This absence of subordination of his political thought to any theological framework is another sign of the challenge of the Gandhian disobedient mind to the concepts and values of the general political order. That is why Gandhi belongs to none of the three ideological options which are available for us today. One option is the return to a 'religious dogmatism'. The second option is 'relativism' which is exemplified by the postmodernist movement that believes that the objective truth should be replaced by hermeneutic truth. The third option is the 'rationalist fundamentalism' which believes in the total power of reason and desacralizes and disenchants everything substantive. Gandhi belongs to none of these three main visions influential at present. He is not a religious fundamentalist. He is not a cultural revivalist, and he is not committed to the idea of absolute reason. What strikes everyone who reads or applies the Gandhian philosophy of disobedience is how he kept a space in his mind open for doubt and for skeptical irony (and even self-irony). In this sense, the moral and political principles of Mahatma Gandhi do not constitute a sort of real gearbox that drives our thought and action in one direction, and is powered by a spiritual engine with only a monolithic ideology as the fuel source. Gandhi had the courage to stand and talk back to the authority of the tradition, being consistent with his beliefs, but at the same time, by remaining free enough to change his mind, discover new things and rediscover what he had once put aside. As a matter of fact, one of the tasks of the Gandhian nonviolence is the effort to breakdown the stereotypes and reductive categories that are limiting to human communication.

Every modern thinker has an audience and a constituency. The issue is whether that audience is there to be flattered and justified, or whether it is to be challenged, and hence, guided into a degree of enlightened maturity. In this respect, the contribution of Mahatma Gandhi in the creation and cultivation of a public culture of disobedience, that guarantees to everyone the right to challenge laws and institutions, and as a strong alternative to a monolithic establishment based on bureaucratic parties and state structures, is one of the most relevant issues to be discussed in political philosophy today. Gandhi was very conscious about the fact that the cultivation of a philosophy of resistance requires the creation of modes of thought and action, where dissenting voices and diverse perspectives could be heard, articulated and put into practice. The Gandhian perspective of dissent invites anyone who cares about the future of freedom in our humanity to ask oneself and others: What does it mean to be a disobedient mind? Assuredly, no one will come first in this intellectual process initiated by Socrates in Athens in the fifth century B.C. Thinking as a mode of questioning is tough stuff; and no wonder our world has difficulty in thinking, questioning and disobeying.

Our age is the age of knowing without questioning. Paradoxically, all the knowledge and information that we have today does not help us to transform and transcend ourselves. We do not experience transcendence in our common lives. That is something which is not pre-given, but needs to be realized as a task in the process of searching and becoming. We perfect our spirit with each moment of reflection and action, and we do this always starting anew. As John Dewey says, 'Travelling is a constant arriving.'[131] This constant move forward means modifying established beliefs and inherited social institutions that prove unsuitable for our new historical stage of consciousness and new cultural and political demands. Paolo Freire, the Brazilian pedagogue, calls this move beyond the naïve awareness of the world as 'conscientization' (*conscientizacao*). Freire explains, 'Conscientization implies...that when I realize that I am oppressed, I know I can liberate myself if I transform the concrete situation where I find myself oppressed...[This] implies a critical insertion into a process, it implies a historical commitment to make changes.'[132] Following Freire's view, conscientization is an act of disobedience dedicated to changing the world and making it more humane, so as to restore empathy between humans and between humankind and the planet Earth. As such, we need to disobey the dehumanizing world of having, in order to enter the collaborative and interconnected world of being. Arguably, this is seen by a thinker like Dewey as contributing to a meaningful whole. Dewey's emphasis on collaborative living exists in order to maintain perpetual social change and promote hopeful citizenship. As Dewey puts it, 'A democracy is more than a form of government; it is primarily a mode of associated living, of conjoint communicated experience.'[133] In sum, for a thinker like Dewey, as for Gandhi, to live in hope is to change our view of the world. No matter how different we are, we remain part of a human community. In *A Common Faith*, Dewey captures the essence of this interconnectedness: 'The things in civilization we most prize are not of ourselves. They exist by grace of the doings and sufferings of the continuous human community in which we are a link. Ours is the responsibility of conserving, transmitting, rectifying and expanding the heritage of values we have received, that those who come after us may receive it more solid and secure, more widely accessible and more generously shared than we have received it. Here are all the elements for a religious faith that shall not be confined to sect, class or race. Such a faith has always been implicitly the common faith of mankind. It remains to make it explicit and militant.'[134]

In short, adopting democratic thinking and its practices to all departments of life is another way to urge for a life of disobedience, challenge and creativity. There is a good reason to believe that dissent and disobedience are not only necessary for the intellectual life of nations, but it is also a universal condition of the coming into the existence of the better of humanity. This is one reason for maintaining a life of dissent as against the rise of mediocrity in the contemporary world.

A second reason would be to integrate the

failures and successes of living in truth by overruling both existentialist hopelessness and the utilitarian illusion of great happiness. True, existence is a tale told by an idiot full of sound and fury, but it is also a tale of struggle for freedom and resistance against evil. The central reason for the vitality of Gandhian ideas, but also those of many other dissenter-thinkers is the aspiration for a world of free human beings and free societies. The problem of freedom could not be isolated from the social, political and cultural conditions which nourish or kill freedom. In our concern with freedom in our contemporary world, we must do more than worry over governmental obstructions of freedom. Once again, as Dewey suggests, democracy is 'expressed in the attitudes of human beings and is measured by consequences produced in their lives.'[135] The problem of freedom and democracy is, then, the problem of educating free and questioning minds. In one of his major contributions, *Democracy and Education*, John Dewey contends that the moral purpose of a democratic society is the educational growth of individuals who are not subordinate to a fixed system of social, economic and political institutions. In other words, Dewey realizes that education has its important art in the survival of man's freedom. However, Dewey tells us in *Philosophies of Freedom* that freedom is not a fact, it is a possibility. And as any other possibility, it needs to be actualized. 'I sum up by saying that the possibility of freedom is deeply grounded in our very beings,' writes Dewey. 'It is one with our individuality, our being uniquely what we are and not imitators and parasites of others. But unlike all other possibilities, this possibility has to be actualized; and, like all others, it can only be actualized through interaction with objective conditions.... Freedom has too long been thought as an indeterminate power operating in a closed and ended world. In its reality, freedom is a resolute will operating in a world in some respects indeterminate, because it is open and moving toward a new future.'[136] As we can see Dewey's idea of movement towards a new future is expressed by the idea of growth without fixed ends. Many considered wrongly that Dewey's pragmatism is too optimistic. On the contrary, it is a viable philosophy of resistance to authoritarianism and a pedagogic response to our ambient nihilism. Inevitably, the Deweyan critical task of democracy and education, as in the case of the Gandhian philosophy of resistance, guides us in this age of conformist and complacent citizenship out of immaturity and towards the process of questioning. Conformism, in this relativistic picture, presents itself as a reactionary appeal to the acceptance of meaninglessness. Interestingly, Dewey's own criticism of conformism and standardization could be considered as a form of philosophical resistance to the 'tragedy of the lost individual' which results from 'an inner void' and 'vacuum'.[137] Dewey's concern, which is ours in today's world, is the state of 'moral subjection' of the individuals in a system where they are unable any longer to think. This is a society where people can say no more, 'I think, therefore I am' and where individuals live with the fear of repeating 'I doubt, therefore I am'. It is this double fear that warns us of a symptom of murderous nihilism and oblivious conformism in our system of democracy and education.

With these implications for contemporary democracy and education, the process of self-overcoming and self-transformation cannot rely uniquely on the work of populist politicians and behaviourist educators. Certainly, there is a need for transcendence from within. This can be pursued through our engagement with the process of questioning. This questioning seems to be today a non-Western perspective rather than a Western one. Far from being an exercise in nostalgia, it would be an intellectual attempt to sketch the larger contours of a non-Western democratic theory based on an ethics of sharing which holds us firm together and leads us to an essential quality of being. This is the fundamental premise of the Gandhian Swadeshi (self-sufficiency), based on the art of assuming responsibility for one's political environment and not necessarily excluding the otherness of the other. Tagore joins Gandhi in asserting this sentiment of empathy and logic of interconnectedness. In a memorable passage of his *Swadeshi Samaj*, he writes, 'Time has come when our samaj will become a true, all-encompassing swadeshi samaj. Time has come for everyone to think that I am not an isolated unit—no one has the right to abandon me even if I am small, and likewise, I have the responsibility to take care of even the weakest.'[138] Reflecting with considerable depth on this possibility of interconnectedness beyond the blind obedience of the Western view of the political, Tagore provides us with a multi-layered cosmopolitanism which gives a multi-dimensional sense of being in the world. Unlike what we see in our mutilated world today, where in the words of Tagore there is 'a growing totality of happenings that by chance have assumed a particular shape and tendency,'[139] he invites us to elaborate our questioning in terms of a creative and renewed border-crossing. Against the obligation to obey the globalized laws of techno-science and capitalism, Tagore's creative border-crossing carries the weight of an ontological disobedience. More provocatively, Tagore talks about 'the obesity of ugliness in our society' where harmonious exchange is lost 'under the tyranny of a prolific greed, like an overladen market-cart, jolting and creaking on the road that leads from things to the Nothing, tearing ugly ruts across the green life till it breaks down under the burden of its vulgarity on the wayside, reaching nowhere.'[140]

This brings us to the ending question of this book for which the previous pages prepared the ground: how could we reject the dominating norms of a decivilized world and return to 'humanity', in the Kantian sense of the term, as an end and never as a means in itself, which emerges from its self-incurred immaturity? We can think in terms of the disobedient mind as the assertion of humanity's adulthood and its rebellion against all external authority outside its autonomy. But it seems that in order to explore its ways of intellectual maturity, humanity needs to contextualize the Gandhian philosophy of dissent to the present situation of the world. To imbibe the philosophy of dissent in a world plagued by conformism seems like a Herculean task to everyone. And yet, we need to take some preliminary steps to put this into practice. Learning to disobey unjust laws which are presented by today's politicians as just and legitimate is not an easy task. If we want to practise democracy in a new manner, we need to think the political in a new fashion.

This is what Mahatma Gandhi does beyond all the thinkers and practitioners of the twentieth century. Gandhi never proclaimed that he was writing on politics per se, but that he was interested in experimenting with truth. As such, whether or not his reflections on the politics of his time was an analysis of the political, his method was revolutionary. Maybe, that is why the Gandhian philosophy of dissent is as potent and controversial today as it ever was. Today, many decades after Gandhi's assassination, the Gandhian moment of the political undoubtedly plays a crucial role in responding to the shortcomings of democratic passion and inclusive governance in our world.

Assuredly, critical disobedience, in comparison to blind and conformist obedience, may better and more humanely protect and advance justice. So, if law and lawmaking is always on the side of the State, on the contrary, justice is always within nonviolent civil society and among its civic actors. As such, we need, more than ever, to revive the traditions of disobedience in the West and the East, as those of Henry David Thoreau and Mahatma Gandhi, which point acidly to the authoritarian norms and hierarchical systems of thought in our world. Here, any theoretical or practical resorting to nonviolence would appear as a key turning point in the understanding and transformation of the political realm. The values of such nonviolent forms of ethical resistance are based on the heroic act of speaking dissent to power and exposing one's disobeying voice. And if we do not have yet this disobeying voice, it is well worth struggling for it through critical opposition to dominant stereotypes of today's society that rationalize forms of structural injustice.

Let us not forget that, strengthening the resisting voices of otherness helps empower creative forms of moral and political agency. As Arundhati Roy affirms in *War Talk*, 'The world over, nonviolent resistance movements are being crushed and broken. If we do not respect and honor them, by default we privilege those who turn to violent means.'[141] What Roy points out here is the dilemma with which Mahatma Gandhi or Martin Luther King Jr. are confronted: to follow the path of nonviolence or to perish with violence. The choice of nonviolent resistance is a manner of speaking in that universal ethical voice which aims at reforming the social ills and economic injustices in our world. If this were not done, it would be for everyone to do what someone else told them to, instead of following their own conscience. This is a rule that concerns society as a whole as well as each individual in it. Hence, what we understand by the common good of all is not to appeal to the general happiness of individuals in a society which is enchained by obedience to a political framework which refuses to be criticized and changed. From the standpoint of the Gandhian theory of dissent, we can only say that one has, not only the political right but the moral duty, to engage in nonviolent disobedience, in order to threaten the mediocrity and immaturity of a society which refuses to think critically and act responsibly. This is a self-transforming temperament which needs to be injected in the veins of contemporary democracies. Therefore, far from being a utopian dream, democratization of democracies is a blueprint for a new space of autonomy and non-demagogic politics. This is precisely the undercurrent in the politics of dissent that we need to uncover.

But all this is by no means the end of the political. As history consistently demonstrates, with domination comes dissent and with restraint comes resistance. As Martin Luther King Jr. underlined in his last interview in 25 March 1968, practically ten days before his assassination, 'with this coalition of conscience we will be able to get something moving again....'[142] In choosing such an ethical imperative, the political becomes, once again, a foundation of and for our times.

With Gandhi, human conscience finally returns to earth, to the here and now, after centuries of temptation looking for salvation in eschatological constructions. Gandhi knew well that one cannot be a friend of Truth without living on the edge. For him, therefore, thinking critically and living radically became one. Thanks to his heretic mind, he always thought differently and lived marginally. His opening up to the world went hand in hand with his act of being free. While listening to his inner voice, he also had an acute sense of the world. Gandhi preferred to walk with others on a tightrope, free of prejudice, complacency and mediocrity, rather than walking alone on rigid, inflexible and impenetrable political and cultural grounds. This is his legacy of heresy and disobedience, which is needed now more than ever.

NOTES

Introduction: The Obligation to Disobey

1. Henry David Thoreau, 'Civil Disobedience,' in *Civil Disobedience: Theory and Practice*, ed. Hugo Adam Bedau (New York: Pegasus, 1969), 28.
2. Ibid., 35.
3. George Woodcock, *Civil Disobedience* (Toronto: Canadian Broadcasting Company, 1969), 69.
4. Ibid., 34.
5. Ibid., 47.
6. Quoted in Walter Harding, *The Variorum Civil Disobedience* (New York: Twayne Publishers, 1967), 74.
7. Cornelius Castoriadis, *Philosophy, Politics, Autonomy*, ed. D.A. Curtis (Oxford: Oxford University Press, 1991), 165.
8. Ibid., 164.
9. Cornelius Castoriadis, *World in Fragments* (Palo Alto: Stanford University Press, 1997), 87.
10. Quoted in Alexandros Kioupkiolis, *Freedom After the Critique of Foundations: Marx, Liberalism, Castoriadis and Agonistic Autonomy* (New York: Palgrave, 2012), 202.
11. Quoted in A.J. Muste, 'Of Holy Disobedience,' in

Civil Disobedience: Theory and Practice, ed. Hugo Adam Bedau, 35.

1. A Disobedient Mind

12. Martin Heidegger, *What Is Called Thinking?* (New York: Harper & Row Publishers, 1968), 5–6.
13. Ibid., 185.
14. Ibid., 5.
15. Cass R. Sunstein, *Why Societies Need Dissent* (Vol. 9) (Cambridge, MA: Harvard University Press, 2005), 81.
16. Albert Camus, *The Rebel* (New York: Vintage Books, 1991), 14.
17. Karl Jaspers, *Man in the Modern Age* (New York: Anchor Books, 1957), 159.
18. Vaclav Havel, *Disturbing the Peace: A Conversation with Karel Hvizdala* (New York: Vintage Books, 1991), 167.
19. Martin Luther King Jr., 'Love, Law and Civil Disobedience,' in *A Testament of Hope: The Essential Writings and Speeches of Martin Luther King, Jr.*, ed. James M. Washington (San Francisco: Harper San Francisco, 1986), 47.
20. Jaspers, *Man in the Modern Age*, 228.
21. Ibid., 8–9.
22. Erich Fromm, *Man for Himself: An Inquiry into the Psychology of Ethics* (Oxon: Routledge, 1947), 248.
23. Ibid., 26–7.
24. Ibid., 161.
25. Ibid., 25–6.
26. Ibid., 207.
27. Jaspers, *Man in the Modern Age*, 116.
28. Quoted in Erich Fromm, *Man for Himself*, 38.

2. Questioning the Political

29. Hannah Arendt, *The Promise of Politics* (New York: Schocken Books, 2005), 190.
30. Ibid., 115.
31. Camus, *The Rebel*, 139.
32. Hannah Arendt, *The Portable Hannah Arendt*, ed. Peter Baehr (New York: Penguin Books, 2000), 16.
33. Hannah Arendt, *Between Past and Future: Eight Exercises in Political Thought* (New York: The Viking Press, 1968), 153.
34. Hannah Arendt, *The Portable Hannah Arendt*, 183.
35. Moya K. Mason, 'Hesiod's Theogony, Myths and Meaning' accessed on 8 March 2014. http://www.moyak.com/papers/hesiod-theogony.html.
36. Cornelius Castoriadis, *Philosophy, Politics, Autonomy*, ed. David Ames Curtis, 159.
37. Ibid., 160–1.
38. Ibid.
39. Thucydides, *The Peloponnesian War* (Book 2.34-46) in http://legacy.fordham.edu/halsall/ancient/pericles-funeralspeech.asp
40. Sara S. Monoson, *Plato's Democratic Entanglements: Athenian Politics and the Practice of Philosophy* (Princeton: Princeton University Press, 2000), 8.
41. Francesco Citti, 'Nature and Natural Law in Roman Declamation,' in *Law and Ethics in Greek and Roman Declamation*, eds Eugenio Amato, Francesco Citti, Bart Huelsenbeck (Munich: De Gruyter, 2015), 106.

42. Natalie Riendeau, *The Legendary Past: Michael Oakeshott on Imagination and Political Identity* (Exeter: Imprint Academic, 2014).

43. David Wiles, *Theatre and Citizenship: The History of a Practice* (Cambridge: Cambridge University Press, 2011), 12.

44. Paul Weithman, 'Augustine's Political Philosophy,' in *The Cambridge Companion to Augustine*, eds Eleonore Stump and Norman Kretzmann (Cambridge: Cambridge University Press, 2006), 245–8.

45. Cornelius Castoriadis, 'The Greek *Polis* and the Creation of Democracy,' in *The Castoriadis Reader*, ed. and trans. David Ames Curtis (Oxford: Blackwell Publishers, 1997), 282.

46. Hannah Arendt, *The Human Condition* (Chicago: University of Chicago Press, 1958), 199.

47. Castoriadis, 'The Greek *Polis* and the Creation of Democracy,' 271.

48. Chantal Mouffe, *On the Political* (London: Routledge, 2005), 9.

49. Ibid., 31.

50. Claude Lefort, *Democracy and Political Theory* (Cambridge: Polity Press, 1988), 181.

51. Alexis de Tocqueville, *Democracy in America* (Vol. II.), 214.

3. The Unholy Crowds: Docility and Obedience

52. Wilhelm Reich, *The Mass Psychology of Fascism* (Harmondsworth: Penguin, 1975), 53.

53. Etienne de La Boétie, *The Politics of Obedience* (New York: Free Life Editions, 1975), 48.

54. Ibid., 68.

55. Etienne de La Boétie, *The Discours sur la servitude volontaire*, (New York: Columbia University Press, 1942), 54.

56. Elias Canetti, *Crowds and Power* (New York: Farrar, Strauss and Giroux, 1984), 311.

57. Ibid., 297.

58. Mouffe, *On the Political*, 13.

59. Michel Foucault, *The Courage of Truth* (Hampshire: Palgrave Macmillan, 2011), 6–7.

60. Ibid., 11.

61. Canetti, *Crowds and Power*, 15–16.

62. Niccolo Machiavelli, *The Discourses* (Harmondsworth: Penguin, 1970), 25.

63. Arendt, *The Human Condition*, 57.

64. Ibid., 58.

65. Guy Debord, *The Society of the Spectacle*, trans. David Nicholson-Smith (New York: Zone Books, 1994), 1.

66. Ibid., 9.

67. Ibid., 58.

68. Walter Lipmann, 'The Phantom Public,' in *The Idea of Public Sphere: A Reader*, eds Gripsrud, Moe, Molander and Murdock (Maryland: Lexington Books, 2010), 25.

69. Ibid., 25.

70. Carl Schmitt, *The Crisis of Parliamentary Democracy*, trans. Ellen Kennedy (Cambridge: MIT Press, 1985), 6.

71. Ibid., 34.

72. Heinrich Meier, *The Lesson of Carl Schmitt* (Chicago: University of Chicago Press, 1998), 45–6.

73. Ibid., 46.

74. Cornelius Castoriadis, '"Paideia" and Democracy,' *Counterpoints* 422 (2012): 72.

75. Ibid.

76. Neeladri Bhattacharya, 'Notes Towards a Conception of the Colonial Public' in *Civil Society, Public Sphere and Citizenship*, eds Bhargava, Helmut, Reifeld, (New Delhi: Sage Publications, 2005), 139.

77. Immanuel Kant, Kant's *Gesammelte Schriften* (Vol. 5), ed. Preussischen Akademie der Wissenschaften (Berlin: Walter de Gruyter, 1900), 431.

78. Quoted in Felicitas G. Munzel, 'Kant on Moral Education, or 'Enlightenment' and the Liberal Arts,' *Review of Metaphysics* 57, no. 1 (2003): 43.

79. Castoriadis, '"Paideia" and Democracy,' 80.

4. Gandhi and the Imperative of Dissent

80. Cited in Arvind Sharma, *Gandhi: A Spiritual Biography* (New Haven: Yale University Press, 2013), 4–5.

81. Richard Sorabji, *Gandhi and the Stoics: Modern Experiments in Ancient Values* (Chicago: University of Chicago Press, 2012), 1.

82. M.K. Gandhi, *The Collected Works of Mahatma Gandhi (in 100 Volumes)* Vol. 7 (New Delhi: Publication Division, Government of India), 267.

83. Ibid., Vol. 9, 183.

84. Raghavan N. Iyer, 'Raghavan N. Iyer on Gandhi,' in *Civil Disobedience* (Santa Barbara: The Center for the Study of Democratic Institutions, 1966), 21.

85. Gandhi, *Collected Works* Vol. 7, 218.

86. Ibid., Vol. 56, 182.

87. Ibid., Vol. 68, 259.
88. Anthony J. Parel, *Gandhi's Philosophy and the Quest for Harmony* (Cambridge: Cambridge University Press, 2006), 199–200.
89. Cited in Dennis Dalton, *Mahatma Gandhi: Nonviolent Power in Action* (New York: Columbia University Press, 1993), 194.
90. M.K. Gandhi, *Satyagraha in South Africa* (Ahmedabad: Navajivan Publishing House, 1928), 105–6.
91. A.J. David Richards, *Disarming Manhood: Roots of Ethical Resistance* (Athens, Ohio: Swallow Press, 2005), 112.
92. Bhikhu Parekh, *Colonialism, Tradition and Reform: An Analysis of Gandhi's Political Discourse* (New Delhi: Sage Publications, 1999), 84.
93. Bakhyt Kadyrova, 'Gandhi's Ideas on Ideal Society and Its Law,' in *Revisiting Gandhi*, ed. R.P. Dwivedi (New Delhi: Radha Publications, 2007), 27.
94. Bhikhu Parekh, *Gandhi* (Oxford: Oxford University Press, 1997), 90.
95. Gandhi, *Collected Works* Vol. 72, 202.
96. Ibid., Vol. 58, 374–5.
97. Cited in John A. Simmons, *Moral Principles and Political Obligation* (Princeton: Princeton University Press, 1981), 200.
98. Bakhyt Kadyrova, 'Gandhi's Ideas on Ideal Society and its Law,' 29.
99. Ibid.
100. Gandhi, *Collected Works*, Vol. 83, 208.
101. M.K. Gandhi, *The Essential Writings* (Oxford: Oxford University Press, 2008), 299-300.

102. Ibid., 301.
103. Gandhi, *Collected Works*, Vol. 51, 59.
104. Sunil Khilnani, *The Idea of India* (New York: Farrar, Straus and Giroux, 1999), 164–5.
105. Parel, *Gandhi's Philosophy and the Quest for Harmony*, 72.

5. The Disobedient Indian

106. Gandhi, *The Essential Writings*, 366–7.
107. Sorabji, *Gandhi and the Stoics*, 199.
108. Ibid., 10–11.
109. Anthony J. Parel, *Pax Gandhiana* (Oxford: Oxford University Press, 2016), 11.
110. Gandhi, *The Essential Writings*, 149.
111. Ibid., 151–2.
112. Gandhi, *The Collected Works* Vol. 45, 269.
113. Gandhi, *Hind Swaraj and Other Writings* (Cambridge: Cambridge University Press, 1997), 116.
114. Ibid., 71.
115. David Hardiman, *Gandhi in His Times and Ours: The Global Legacy of His Ideas* (New York: Columbia University Press, 2003), 26.
116. Camus, *The Rebel*, 285.
117. Paul F. Power, 'Mahatma Gandhi and Civil Disobedience,' in *The Meanings of Gandhi*, ed. Paul F. Power (Honolulu: University Press of Hawaii, 1971), 175.
118. Gandhi, *The Essential Writings*, 373.
119. Ibid., 373.
120. Louis Fischer, *A Week with Gandhi* (London: George Allen and Unwin, 1943), 96–7.

121. Martin Luther King Jr., 'Where Do We Go From Here?' in *A Testament of Hope: The Essential Writings and Speeches of Martin Luther King Jr.*, 629.

Conclusion:
Towards a Gandhian Philosophy of Dissent

122. M.K. Gandhi, *All Men Are Brothers* (New York: Continnum, 2011), 138.

123. Vaclav Havel, 'The Power of the Powerless,' in *Open Letters: Selected Prose 1965–90* (London: Faber and Faber, 1991), 136.

124. Ibid.

125. Ibid., 43.

126. Gandhi, *All Men Are Brothers*, 84–5.

127. Martin Luther King Jr., 'MIA Mass Meeting at Holt Street Baptist Church,' in *The Papers of Martin Luther King, Jr.: Birth of a New Age, December 1955–56 (Vol. 3)*, eds Clayborne Carson, Steward Burns, Susan Carson, et al. (Berkeley: University of California Press, 1997), 71.

128. Cited in Margaret Chatterjee, *Gandhi and the Challenge of Religious Diversity: Religious Pluralism Revisited* (New Delhi: Promilla & Co. Publishers, 2005), 315.

129. Gandhi, *The Collected Works*, Vol. 21, 246.

130. Ibid.

131. John Dewey, 'Human Nature and Conduct,' in *The Collected Works of John Dewey [1899–1924]*, ed. Jo Ann Boydston (Illinois: Southern Illinois University Press, 1983), 195.

132. Paulo Freire, 'Conscientizing as a Way of Liberating,'

LADOC, A Documentation Service of the Division of Latin America—USCC, II, 29a, April, 1972, 5.

133. John Dewey, 'The Democratic Conception in Education,' in *The Middle Works of John Dewey [1899–1924]*, ed. Jo Ann Boydston (Illinois: Southern Illinois University Press, 1980), 93.

134. Cited in Stephen M. Fishman and Lucille McCarthy, *John Dewey and the Philosophy and Practice of Hope* (Chicago: University of Illinois Press, 2007), 7.

135. John Dewey, *Freedom and Culture* (New York: G. P. Putnam's Sons, 1939), 125.

136. Dewey, 'Philosophies of Freedom,' in *On Experience, Nature and Freedom: Representative Selections*, ed. Richard J. Bernstein (New York: Liberal Arts Press, 1960), 287.

137. Dewey, 'Individualism Old and New,' in *The Later Works of John Dewey* Vol. 5, ed. Jo Ann Boydston (Carbondale: Southern Illinois University Press, 1984), 83.

138. Cited in Rustom Bharucha, *Another Asia: Rabindranath Tagore & Okakura Tenshin* (New Delhi: Oxford University Press, 2006), 61–2.

139. See Rabindranath Tagore, *Talks in China* (New Delhi: Rupa & Company, 2002), 118.

140. Rabindranath Tagore, 'Civilisation and Progress,' in *Rabindranath Tagore: Selected Essays* (New Delhi: Rupa & Company, 2004), 279.

141. Arundhati Roy, *War Talk* (Cambridge, MA: South End Press, 2003), 13.

142. Martin Luther King Jr., *The Last Interview: and Other Conservations* (New York: Melville House, 2017), 115.

REFERENCES

Arendt, Hannah. *Between Past and Future: Eight Exercises in Political Thought*. New York: The Viking Press, 1968.

—— *The Human Condition*. Chicago: University of Chicago Press, 1958.

—— *The Portable Hannah Arendt*, edited by Peter Baehr. New York: Penguin Books, 2000.

—— *The Promise of Politics*. New York: Schocken Books, 2005.

Bharucha, Rustom. *Another Asia: Rabindranath Tagore & Okakura Tenshin*. New Delhi: Oxford University Press, 2006.

Bhattacharya, Neeladri. 'Notes Towards a Conception of the Colonial Public.' In *Civil Society, Public Sphere and Citizenship*, Edited by Bhargava, Helmut and Reifeld, 130–56. New Delhi: Sage Publications, 2005.

Boétie, Etienne de La. *The Politics of Obedience*. New York: Free Life Editions, 1975.

—— *The Discours sur la servitude volontaire*. New York: Columbia University Press, 1942.

Camus, Albert. *The Rebel*. New York: Vintage Books, 1991.

Canetti, Elias. *Crowds and Power*. Translated by Carol Stewart. New York: Farrar, Straus and Giroux, 1984.

Castoriadis, Cornelius. 'The Greek *Polis* and the Creation of Democracy,' In *The Castoriadis Reader*, Edited and translated by David Ames Curtis. Oxford: Blackwell Publishers, 1997.

———"'Paideia' and Democracy." *Counterpoints* 422 (2012): 71–80.

———*Philosophy, Politics, Autonomy*, Edited by D.A. Curtis. Oxford: Oxford University Press, 1991.

——— *World in Fragments*. Palo Alto: Stanford University Press, 1997.

Chatterjee, Margaret. *Gandhi and the Challenge of Religious Diversity: Religious Pluralism Revisited*. New Delhi: Promilla & Co. Publishers, 2005.

Citti Francesco. 'Nature and Natural Law in Roman Declamation.' In *Law and Ethics in Greek and Roman Declamation*, Edited by Eugenio Amato, Francesco Citti, Bart Huelsenbeck. Munich: De Gruyter, 2015.

Dalton, Dennis. *Mahatma Gandhi: Nonviolent Power in Action*. New York: Columbia University Press, 1993.

Debord, Guy. *The Society of the Spectacle*. Translated by Donald Nicholson-Smith. New York: Zone Books, 1994.

Dewey, John. *Democracy and Education: An Introduction to the Philosophy of Education*. New York: Macmillan, 1916.

———*Freedom and Culture*. New York: G.P. Putnam's Sons, 1939.

———'Human Nature and Conduct.' In *The Collected Works of John Dewey [1899-1924]*, Edited by Jo Ann Boydston. Illinois: Southern Illinois University Press, 1983.

——— 'Individualism Old and New.' In *The Collected Works of John Dewey* Vol. 5, Edited by Jo Ann Boydston. Carbondale: Southern Illinois University Press, 1984.

——— 'Philosophies of Freedom.' In *On Experience, Nature and Freedom: Representative Selections*, Edited by Richard J. Bernstein. New York: Liberal Arts Press, 1960.

——— 'The Democratic Conception in Education.' In *The Middle Works of John Dewey [1899-1924]*, Edited by Jo Ann Boydston. Illinois: Southern Illinois University Press, 1980.

Fischer, Louis. *A Week with Gandhi*. London: George Allen and Unwin, 1943.

Fishman, Stephen, and Lucille McCarthy. *John Dewey and the Philosophy and Practice of Hope*. Chicago: University of Illinois Press, 2007.

Foucault, Michel. *The Courage of Truth*. Hampshire: Palgrave Macmillan, 2011.

Freire, Paulo, 'Conscientizing as a Way of Liberating,' LADOC, A Documentation Service of the Division of Latin America—*USCC*, II, 29a, April, 1972, 4 pages (mimeographed).

Fromm, Erich. *Man for Himself: An Inquiry into the Psychology of Ethics*. Oxon: Routledge, 1947.

Gandhi, M.K. *All Men Are Brothers*. New York: Continuum, 2011.

——— *The Collected Works of Mahatma Gandhi (in 100 Volumes)*. New Delhi: Publication Division, Government of India.

——— *The Essential Writings*. Oxford: Oxford University Press, 2008.

———— *Hind Swaraj and Other Writings*. Cambridge: Cambridge University Press, 1997.

———— *Satyagraha in South Africa*. Ahmedabad: Navajivan Publishing House, 1928.

Hardiman, David. *Gandhi in His Times and Ours: The Global Legacy of His Ideas*. New York: Columbia University Press, 2003.

Harding, Walter Roy. *The Variorum Civil Disobedience*. New York: Twayne Publishers, 1967.

Havel, Vaclav. *Disturbing the Peace: A Conversation with Karel Hvizdala*. New York: Vintage Books, 1991.

———— 'The Power of the Powerless.' In *Open Letters: Selected Prose 1965–1990*. London: Faber and Faber, 1991.

Heidegger, Martin. *What Is Called Thinking?*. New York: Harper & Row Publishers, 1968.

Iyer, Raghavan N. 'Raghavan N. Iyer on Gandhi.' In *Civil Disobedience*. Santa Barbara: The Center for the Study of Democratic Institutions, 1966.

Jaspers, Karl. *Man in the Modern Age*. New York: Anchor Books, 1957.

Kadyrova, Bakhyt. 'Gandhi's Ideas on Ideal Society and its Law.' In *Revisiting Gandhi*, Edited by R.P. Dwivedi. New Delhi: Radha Publications, 2007.

Kant, Immanuel. *Kant's Gesammelte Schriften*, Vol. 5, Edited by Preussischen Akademie der Wissenschaften. Berlin: Walter de Gruyter, 1900.

Khilnani, Sunil. *The Idea of India*. New York: Farrar, Straus and Giroux, 1999.

King, Martin Luther Jr. 'Love, Law and Civil Disobedience.' In *A Testament of Hope: The Essential Writings and Speeches of Martin Luther King, Jr.*, Edited by James

M. Washington. San Francisco: Harper San Francisco, 1986.

———'MIA Mass Meeting at Holt Street Baptist Church.' In *The Papers of Martin Luther King, Jr.: Birth of a New Age, December 1955–1956* Vol. 3, Edited by Clayborne Carson, Steward Burns, Susan Carson, et al. Berkeley: University of California Press, 1997.

———'Where Do We Go From Here?' In *A Testament of Hope: The Essential Writings and Speeches of Martin Luther King Jr.*, Edited by James M. Washington. San Francisco: Harper San Francisco, 1986.

———*The Last Interview: and Other Conversations.* New York: Melville House, 2017.

Kioupkiolis, Alexandros. *Freedom After the Critique of Foundations: Marx, Liberalism, Castoriadis and Agonistic Autonomy.* New York: Palgrave, 2012.

Lefort, Claude. *Democracy and Political Theory.* Cambridge: Polity Press, 1988.

Lipmann, Walter. 'The Phantom Public.' In *The Idea of Public Sphere: A Reader*, Edited by Gripsrud, Moe, Molander and Murdock. Maryland: Lexington Books, 2010.

Machiavelli, Niccolo. *The Discourses.* Harmondsworth: Penguin, 1970.

Mason, Moya K. 'Hesiod's Theogony, Myths and Meaning' accessed on 8 March 2014. http://www.moyak. com/papers/hesiod-theogony.html.

Meier, Heinrich. *The Lesson of Carl Schmitt.* Chicago: University of Chicago Press, 1998.

Monoson, Sara S. *Plato's Democratic Entanglements: Athenian Politics and the Practice of Philosophy.* Princeton: Princeton University Press, 2000.

Mouffe, Chantal. *On the Political*. London: Routledge, 2005.

Munzel, G. Felicitas. 'Kant on Moral Education, or "Enlightenment" and the Liberal Arts.' *Review of Metaphysics* 57, no. 1 (2003): 43–73.

Muste, A.J., 'Of Holy Disobedience.' In *Civil Disobedience: Theory and Practice*, Edited by Hugo Adam Bedau. New York: Pegasus, 1969.

Parekh, Bhikhu. *Colonialism, Tradition and Reform: An Analysis of Gandhi's Political Discourse*. New Delhi: Sage Publications, 1999.

——— *Gandhi*. Oxford: Oxford University Press, 1997.

Parel, Anthony J. *Gandhi's Philosophy and the Quest for Harmony*. Cambridge: Cambridge University Press, 2006.

——— *Pax Gandhiana*. Oxford: Oxford University Press, 2016.

Power, Paul F. 'Mahatma Gandhi and Civil Disobedience.' In *The Meanings of Gandhi*, Edited by Paul F. Power. University Press of Hawaii, 1971.

Reich, Wilhelm. *The Mass Psychology of Fascism*. Harmondsworth: Penguin, 1975.

Richards, A.J. David. *Disarming Manhood: Roots of Ethical Resistance*. Athens, Ohio: Swallow Press, 2005.

Riendeau, Natalie. *The Legendary Past: Michael Oakeshott on Imagination and Political Identity*. Exeter: Imprint Academic, 2014.

Roy, Arundhati. *War Talk*. Cambridge, MA: South End Press, 2003.

Schmitt, Carl. *The Crisis of Parliamentary Democracy*. Translated by Ellen Kennedy. Cambridge: MIT Press, 1985.

Sharma, Arvind. *Gandhi: A Spiritual Biography.* New Haven: Yale University Press, 2013.

Simmons, John A., *Moral Principles and Political Obligation.* Princeton: Princeton University Press, 1979.

Sorabji, Richard. *Gandhi and the Stoics: Modern Experiments in Ancient Values.* Chicago: University of Chicago Press, 2012.

Sunstein, Cass R. *Why Societies Need Dissent.* Vol. 9. Cambridge, MA: Harvard University Press, 2005.

Tagore, Rabindranath. 'Civilisation and Progress.' In *Rabindranath Tagore: Selected Essays.* New Delhi: Rupa & Company, 2004.

——— *Talks in China.* New Delhi: Rupa & Company, 2002.

Thoreau, Henry David. 'Civil Disobedience.' In *Civil Disobedience: Theory and Practice*, Edited by Hugo Adam Bedau. New York: Pegasus, 1969.

Thucydides, *The Peloponnesian War* (Book 2.34–46). In http://legacy.fordham.edu/halsall/ancient/pericles-funeralspeech.asp

Tocqueville, Alexis de. *Democracy in America.* John Wiley & Sons, Inc., 1889.

Weithman, Paul. 'Augustine's Political Philosophy.' In *The Cambridge Companion to Augustine*, Edited by Eleonore Stump and Norman Kretzmann. Cambridge: Cambridge University Press, 2001.

Wiles, David. *Theatre and Citizenship: The History of a Practice.* Cambridge: Cambridge University Press, 2011.

Woodcock, George. *Civil Disobedience.* Toronto: Canadian Broadcasting Corp, 1966.

Ramin Jahanbegloo is an Iranian-Canadian philosopher, and the author of twenty-eight books. He is presently the Executive Director and Vice-Dean of the Mahatma Gandhi Centre for Nonviolence and Peace at the Jindal Global University, Delhi. He has worked extensively to foster constructive dialogue between different cultures. In 2006, he was arrested by Iranian authorities on the suspicion of being an American spy. He was released without being charged, after four months of solitary confinement. He is the winner of the Peace Prize from the United Nations Association in Spain (2009) and, more recently, the Josep Palau i Fabre International Essay Prize (2012). Some of his books include *Iran: Between Tradition and Modernity* (2004), *The Spirit of India* (2008), *The Gandhian Moment* (2013), *The Decline of Civilization: Why We Need to Return to Gandhi and Tagore* (2017) and *Letters to a Young Philosopher* (2017).

INDIA DISSENTS: 3,000 YEARS OF DIFFERENCE, DOUBT AND ARGUMENT

Edited and with an Introduction by
Ashok Vajpeyi

'In the long fight for an open society and the full realisation of the fight for the freedom of Indians in a free India, this book will be an invaluable guide.'

—thewire.in

'[This] book makes compelling and mandatory reading…it successfully underlines that India, through its history, has never been a monolithic cultural entity.'

—*Financial Express*

'[This] is a collection that every school principal should be giving as a parting gift to each graduating student.'

—Harish Khare, *The Tribune*

India Dissents: 3,000 Years of Difference, Doubt and Argument brings together some of the voices that have sustained India as a great and vibrant civilization. Collected in these pages are essays, letters, reports, poems, songs and calls to action—from texts ranging from the *Rig Veda* to Ambedkar's *Annihilation of Caste*; and by thinkers as varied as the Buddha, Akka Mahadevi, Lal Ded, Nanak, Ghalib, Tagore, Gandhi, Manto, Jayaprakash Narayan, Namdeo Dhasal, Mahasweta Devi and Amartya Sen. Their words embody the undying and essential spirit of dissent in one of the world's most diverse, dynamic and oldest civilizations.

GANDHI ON NON-VIOLENCE

Edited by Thomas Merton

An essential compendium for understanding
Gandhi's profound legacy.

Gandhi on Non-Violence brings together the political
and moral philosophies central to the life and work of
Mahatma Gandhi, pared down to their essentials.
Philosophies which have influenced generations and
inspired some of the world's most transformative leaders
and its greatest movements; from Martin Luther King, Jr.
and Steve Biko to Václav Havel and Aung San Suu Kyi;
from the Civil Rights movement in America and anti-
apartheid struggles in South Africa to non-violent battles
for democracy in Asia, Latin America and Eastern
Europe.

The principles of ahimsa and satyagraha as practised
by Gandhi were selected for this volume by
Thomas Merton, a theologian, social activist, and one of
the most influential religious thinkers of the twentieth
century. In his comprehensive introduction, Merton
describes ahimsa and satyagraha as not merely political
tools, but a response to evil itself. Which, if followed
with truth and faith, can bring men—and nations—to
their 'right mind' and free them forever from violence.
And emphasizing the universality of ahimsa and
satyagraha, Merton describes how they are linked to the
traditional concept of Hindu dharma, the teachings of
the Greek philosophers Socrates and Plato, and to
Christian thought, especially the act of forgiveness.

Challenging, provocative and eternally valid, Gandhi's
principles are, as Merton himself puts it, 'required reading
for anyone who is seriously interested in man's fate in the
nuclear age.'

www.ingramcontent.com/pod-product-compliance
Lightning Source LLC
Chambersburg PA
CBHW070343270326
41926CB00017B/3953